# You Can Build It

## Book 2

### Table of Contents

# You Can Build It! Book 2

One Very Tired Author, Layout Artist, Designer and Writer: Joe Meno

Publisher and Proofreader: John Morrow

Contributors: Allan Bedford, John Cooper, Christopher Deck, Didier Enjary, Michael Huffman and David Pagano.

Some of the content in *You Can Build It, Book 2* has been previously printed in *BrickJournal* Magazine

Published by:

TwoMorrows Publishing
10407 Bedfordtown Drive
Raleigh, NC 27614
www.twomorrows.com
e-mail: store@twomorrowspubs.com

First Printing: September 2012
Printed in China
ISBN: 978-1-60549-036-6

## Dedication

This book is dedicated to all the builders that have inspired me to build the crazy models I have built, as well as to the builders out there that have yet to step up and create. May they find the inspiration to create at a display, event, or maybe even here.

Dedications also go to my family, who never thought that they would see a son that would end up playing for a career!

And thank you for reading this far... now go build!

*Joe Meno*

## Acknowledgements

Many thanks to the contributors who added their creations to *BrickJournal* and here. Thanks also to the LDraw community for the software it makes available to the community, which we use for making all of the instructions and renderings in this book. We would especially like to thank Kevin Clague for his continued upgrades of the LPub tool that is a part of the LDraw suite. For more information, please visit http://www.ldraw.org.

Also thanks to the gang at the LEGO Group that have helped the community and *BrickJournal* past and present, including Tormod Askildsen, Jan Beyer, Jim Foulds, Jake McKee, Steve Witt, Kevin Hinkle, Peter Espersen, and of course Jørgen Vig Knudstorp and Kjeld Kirk Kristiansen!

### Glossary

**AFOL** (Adult Fan of LEGO)
**NLSO** (Non-LEGO Significant Other)
**MOC** (My Own Creation)
**TLG** (The LEGO Group)
**BURP** (Big Ugly Rock Piece)
**LURP** (Little Ugly Rock Piece)
**POOP** (Pieces—that can be or should be made—Of Other Pieces)
**SNOT** (Studs Not on Top)
**LUG** (LEGO Users Group)
**LTC** (LEGO Train Club)

# Welcome...

...to the second volume of the You Can Build It series of books. Originally, these were going to be compilations of the instructions from *BrickJournal* magazine, but the series changed as it was being designed.

The book became a series of instruction books that went up in levels, from beginner to intermediate to expert. *BrickJournal's* instructions are for beginner to intermediate builders interested in building new things. These books are a more focused document to show building.

One thing that is a common thread in these models is that they use mostly common parts, so hopefully you will have many of the parts needed for a model already in the sets you have bought. If not, the parts lists have the information you need to find any missing parts online. If you want a complete list of the all parts used in this book (including information on identifying, finding, and ordering parts), you can download it at: *http://www.twomorrows.com/media/YouCanBuildIt2List.pdf*

If you don't have internet access and want a hardcopy of the list, send a self-addressed stamped envelope to:

*You Can Build It Parts List*
*TwoMorrows Publishing*
*10407 Bedfordtown Drive*
*Raleigh, NC 27614*

Most of the models here use basic building techniques, so this is a good start into LEGO building. There are some advanced techniques that are used in the larger models, so take a close look at the instructions if there are any problems. The techniques shown in the models are a good look at how you can make a model a certain shape or function a certain way. The scales of the models are a variety, so you have a chance to build an assortment of items, from an military truck to a robot.

When it became apparent that the book would have to have models of a specific skill level, I took a look at my creation library. I have built LEGO models for over ten years, and still have some of my models, which are included here.

Other contributors include people from all around — Christopher Deck from Germany, Didier Enjary from France, and John Cooper, Mike Huffman and David Pagano from the US.

Models are arranged in categories: Sculpture (where you will see building techniques), Minifigure scale (if you want to build something for your LEGO figures) and Microscale, so start where you want to and get building!

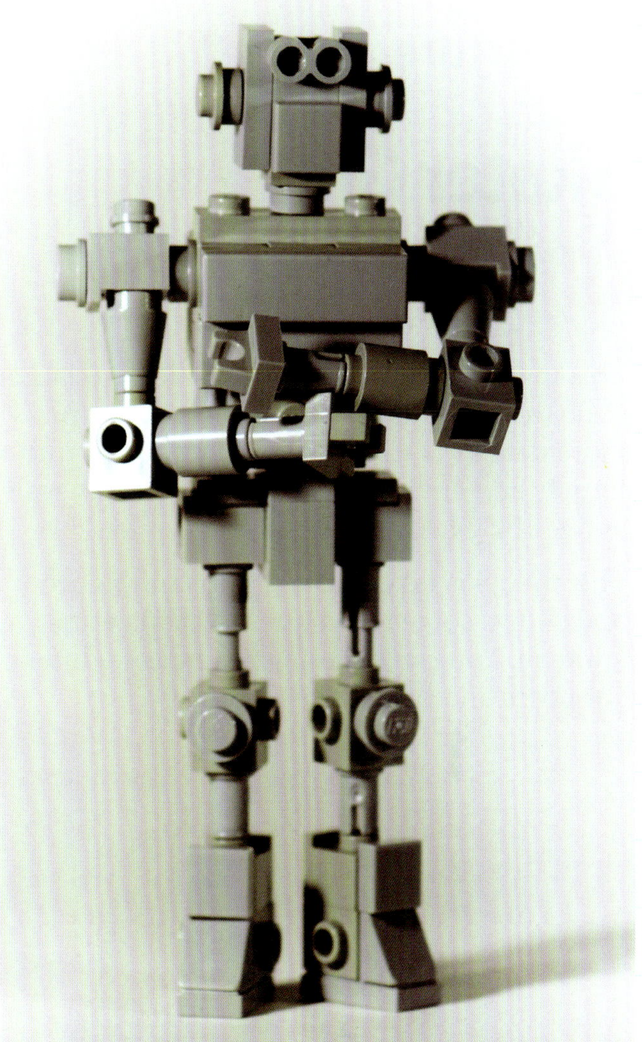

**Don't have all the parts in your collection to build the sets shown in this book? You can download a complete parts list in PDF form, with links to find the ones you need online. Just go to this link:**

**http://www.twomorrows.com/media/YouCanBuildIt2List.pdf**

## Sculpture

# Skater Girl

*Design by Didier Enjary*

*This model first appeared in Issue 7 of* BrickJournal.

This model is Miniland scale, which is a larger scale than minifigure scale. This allows for more detail to be built and incorporated into figures and environments. You'll see this scale at the LEGOLAND park displays.

This model is taken from a Miniland figure and shows some techniques to create arms and hair. You can experiment to create different poses and hair, so give it a try!

*The original model, seen in LEGOLAND.*

## Parts List

*You can find parts on Bricklink.com by searching with the part number.*

| Qty | Part | Description | Color |
|---|---|---|---|
| 1 | 2429.dat | Hinge Plate 1 x 4 Base | Tan |
| 1 | 2430.dat | Hinge Plate 1 x 4 Top | Green |
| 1 | 2431.dat | Tile 1 x 4 with Groove | Brown |
| 2 | 3004.dat | Brick 1 x 2 | Dark Bluish Gray |
| 1 | 3021.dat | Plate 2 x 3 | Green |
| 1 | 3021.dat | Plate 2 x 3 | Dark Bluish Gray |
| 1 | 3022.dat | Plate 2 x 2 | Tan |
| 2 | 3023.dat | Plate 1 x 2 | Black |
| 3 | 3023.dat | Plate 1 x 2 | Tan |
| 1 | 3023.dat | Plate 1 x 2 | Green |
| 1 | 3024.dat | Plate 1 x 1 | Tan |
| 5 | 3062b.dat | Brick 1 x 1 Round with Hollow Stud | Tan |
| 1 | 3069b.dat | Tile 1 x 2 with Groove | Green |
| 2 | 3069b.dat | Tile 1 x 2 with Groove | Tan |
| 1 | 3069b.dat | Tile 1 x 2 with Groove | Dark Bluish Gray |
| 1 | 3665.dat | Slope Brick 45 2 x 1 Inverted | Green |
| 1 | 3700.dat | Technic Brick 1 x 2 with Hole | Brown |
| 2 | 3700.dat | Technic Brick 1 x 2 with Hole | Green |
| 4 | 3794a.dat | Plate 1 x 2 without Groove with 1 Centre Stud | Green |
| 1 | 3794a.dat | Plate 1 x 2 without Groove with 1 Centre Stud | Tan |
| 2 | 3794a.dat | Plate 1 x 2 without Groove with 1 Centre Stud | Dark Bluish Gray |
| 1 | 3794b.dat | Plate 1 x 2 with Groove with 1 Centre Stud | Tan |
| 1 | 3794b.dat | Plate 1 x 2 with Groove with 1 Centre Stud | Green |
| 2 | 4070.dat | Brick 1 x 1 with Headlight | Black |
| 2 | 4081b.dat | Plate 1 x 1 with Clip Light Type 2 | Brown |
| 1 | 4274.dat | Technic Pin 1/2 | Light Bluish Gray |
| 2 | 4274.dat | Technic Pin 1/2 | Light Blue |
| 2 | 4595.dat | Brick 1 x 2 x 0.667 with Studs on Sides | Black |
| 1 | 6141.dat | Plate 1 x 1 Round | Red |
| 2 | 6541.dat | Technic Brick 1 x 1 with Hole | Green |
| 2 | 30039.dat | Tile 1 x 1 with Groove | Black |
| 3 | 30039.dat | Tile 1 x 1 with Groove | Green |
| 2 | 30071.dat | Brick 1 x 1 | Black |

1 1x

2 1x

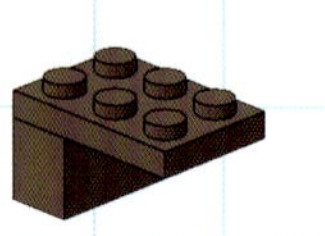

3 1x

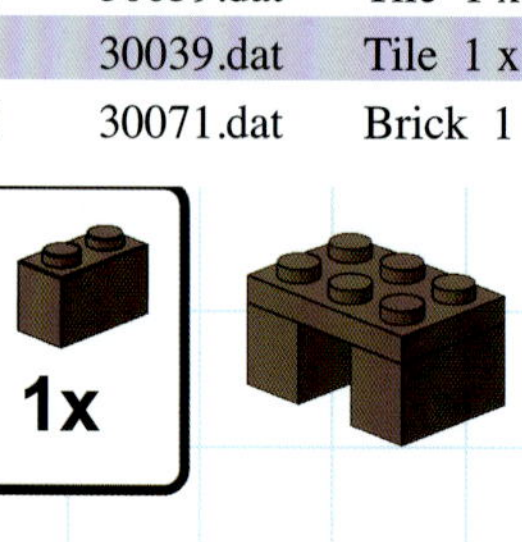

4 2x

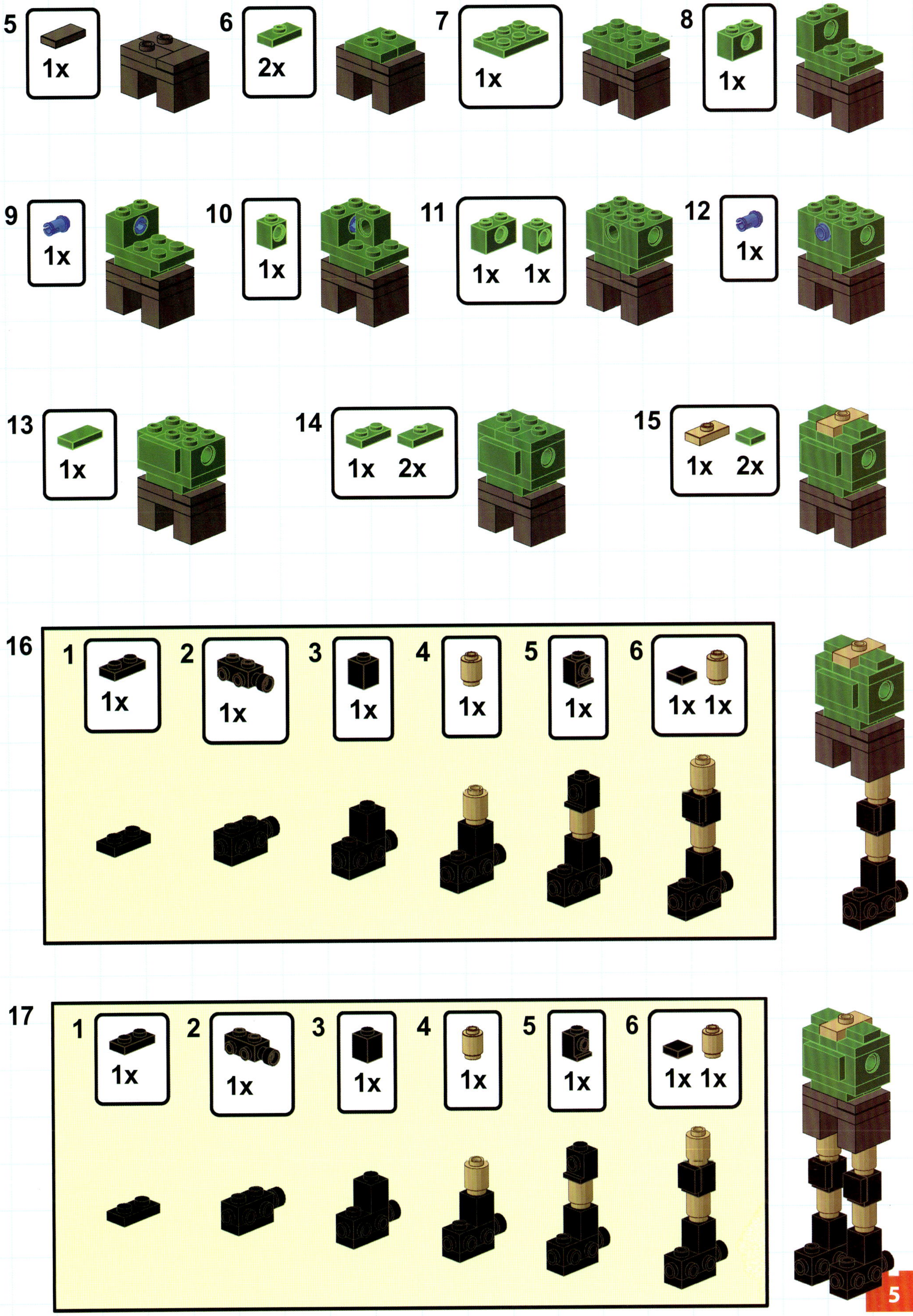

5

1x

6

2x

7

1x

8

1x

9

1x

10

1x

11

1x 1x

12

1x

13

1x

14

1x 2x

15

1x 2x

16

1

1x

2

1x

3

1x

4

1x

5

1x

6

1x 1x

17

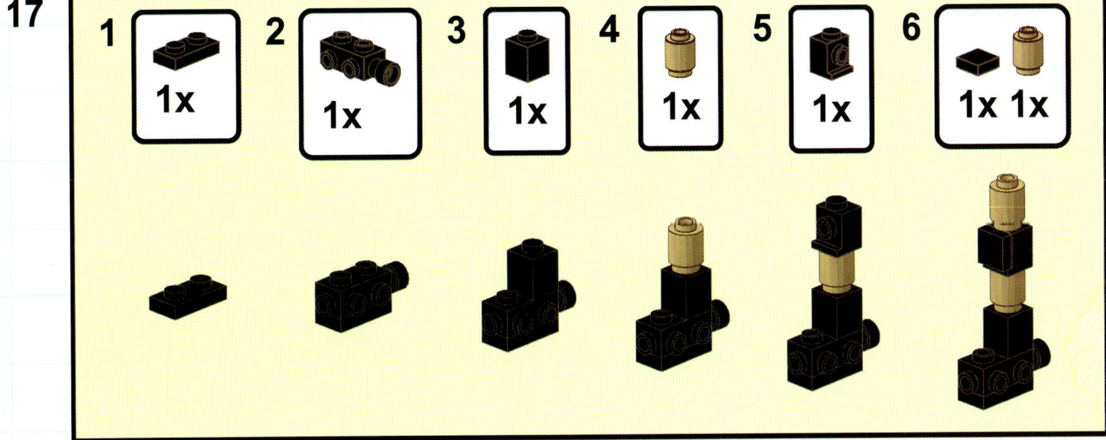

18

1
1x
2
1x
3
1x
4
1x 1x

19

1
1x
2
1x
3
1x 1x

20

1
1x 1x
2
1x
3
1x
4
2x
5
2x
6
1x
7
1x
8
1x

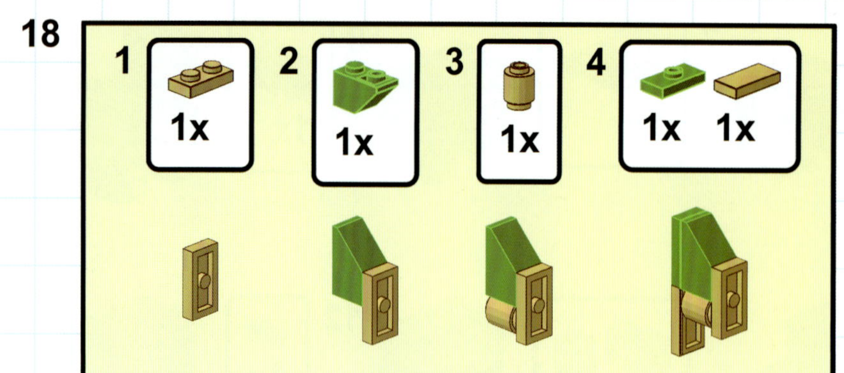

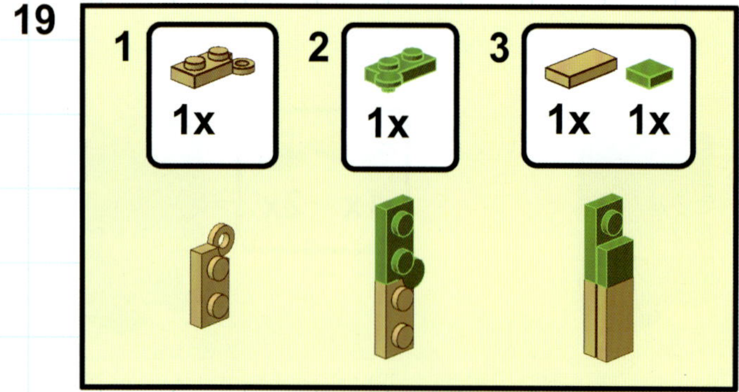

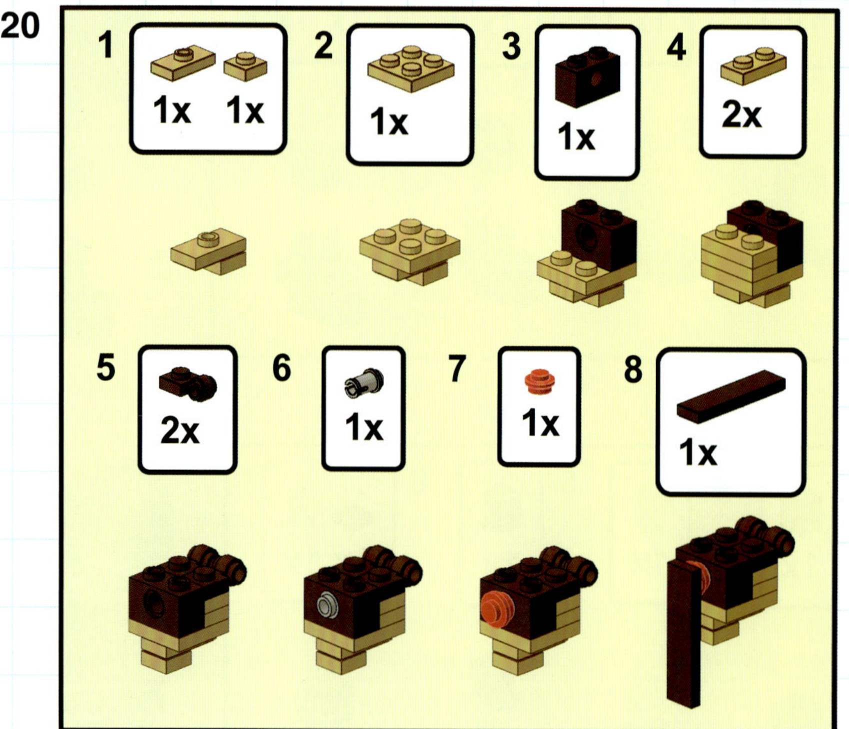

# Animation Puppet



*Model by David Pagano*

*This model first appeared in Issue 14 of* BrickJournal, *which spotlighted brickfilming.*

People tend to use minifigures as the main actors in their LEGO films, but I am continuously fascinated by the possibilities inherent in building my own characters brick by brick.

To that end, this charming fellow is what I call a LEGO animation puppet. He's a refined version of the rig I started experimenting with when I made my film "Playback" in 2008. Back then, I was trying to make do with hiding a lot of Bionicle parts behind regular bricks and plates. I was overjoyed when ball-and-socket joints with studs started popping up in Exo-Force and Power Miners sets. Now we just need them in an assortment of colors...

Anyway, this puppet is about 11.5" tall, and he's got 20 points of articulation (23 if you count his tie). His mouth is built to be removable, and can be replaced with different mouth shapes if you feel ambitious enough for lip-syncing (see the inset photo). He can also be made to blink by placing a couple of 1 x 1 yellow tiles over his eyes for a frame or two.

I purposefully designed this particular character with a bald head and plain clothes; that way, you can customize him to your heart's content. Does he need glasses? A giant sword? A pompadour? I'll leave that up to you. Have fun!

# Parts List

| # | Part | Description | Color |
|---|---|---|---|
| 2 | 3666.dat | Plate 1 x 6 | Black |
| 2 | 6636.dat | Tile 1 x 6 | Black |
| 4 | 3040b.dat | Slope Brick 45 2 x 1 | Black |
| 4 | 3004.dat | Brick 1 x 2 | Black |
| 1 | 32001.dat | Technic Plate 2 x 6 with Holes | Black |
| 2 | 32174.dat | Technic Connector 2 x 3 with Ball Socket | Black |
| 1 | 63868.dat | Plate 1 x 2 with Clip Horizontal on End | Black |
| 1 | 49673.dat | Plate 1 x 1 with Tooth | Black |
| 2 | 3068b.dat | Tile 2 x 2 with Groove | Black |
| 2 | 60478.dat | Plate 1 x 2 with Handle on End | Black |
| 1 | 3794.dat | Plate 1 x 2 with 1 Stud | Black |
| 4 | 32062.dat | Technic Axle 2 Notched | Black |
| 1 | 3623.dat | Plate 1 x 3 | Black |
| 1 | 2555.dat | Tile 1 x 1 with Clip | Black |
| 1 | 32556.dat | Technic Pin Long | Black |
| 2 | 3020.dat | Plate 2 x 4 | Black |
| 4 | 85984.dat | Slope Brick 31 1 x 2 x 0.667 | Black |
| 3 | 3022.dat | Plate 2 x 2 | Black |
| 7 | 3023.dat | Plate 1 x 2 | Black |
| 2 | 3024.dat | Plate 1 x 1 | Black |
| 2 | 6069.dat | Wedge 4 x 4 Triple | Black |
| 1 | 3001.dat | Brick 2 x 4 | Green |
| 2 | 3002.dat | Brick 2 x 3 | Green |
| 1 | 3023.dat | Plate 1 x 2 | Green |
| 1 | 3701.dat | Technic Brick 1 x 4 with Holes | Green |
| 1 | 3010.dat | Brick 1 x 4 | Green |
| 2 | 32062.dat | Technic Axle 2 Notched | Red |
| 2 | 203.dat | Technic Ball Joint | Light Gray |
| 1 | 3709b.dat | Technic Plate 2 x 4 with Holes | Light Gray |
| 4 | 32064b.dat | Technic Brick 1 x 2 with Axlehole Type 2 | Dark Gray |
| 7 | 57909.dat | Brick 2 x 2 with Ball Joint and Axlehole | Dark Gray |
| 2 | 3069b.dat | Tile 1 x 2 with Groove | Dark Gray |
| 1 | 4871.dat | Slope Brick 45 4 x 2 Double Inverted with Open Center | Dark Gray |
| 1 | 57908.dat | Brick 2 x 2 with Two Ball Joints | Dark Gray |
| 2 | 3031.dat | Plate 4 x 4 | Dark Gray |
| 2 | 4859.dat | Wing 3 x 4 with 1 x 2 Cutout without Stud Notches | Dark Gray |
| 8 | 44728.dat | Bracket 1 x 2 - 2 x 2 | Dark Gray |
| 9 | 3020.dat | Plate 2 x 4 | Dark Gray |
| 12 | 3021.dat | Plate 2 x 3 | Dark Gray |
| 6 | 3022.dat | Plate 2 x 2 | Dark Gray |
| 14 | 3023.dat | Plate 1 x 2 | Dark Gray |
| 9 | 62712.dat | Brick 2 x 2 with Ball Socket and Axlehole | Dark Gray |
| 2 | 3665.dat | Slope Brick 45 2 x 1 Inverted | Yellow |
| 2 | 3815c01.dat | Minifig Hips and Legs (Complete) | Yellow |

| # | Part | Description | Color |
|---|---|---|---|
| 2 | 3069b.dat | Tile 1 x 2 with Groove | Yellow |
| 1 | 3001.dat | Brick 2 x 4 | Yellow |
| 2 | 2420.dat | Plate 2 x 2 Corner | Yellow |
| 1 | 3003.dat | Brick 2 x 2 | Yellow |
| 2 | 3040b.dat | Slope Brick 45 2 x 1 | Yellow |
| 4 | 3004.dat | Brick 1 x 2 | Yellow |
| 6 | 3005.dat | Brick 1 x 1 | Yellow |
| 2 | 30039.dat | Tile 1 x 1 with Groove | Yellow |
| 2 | 4070.dat | Brick 1 x 1 with Headlight | Yellow |
| 6 | 3794.dat | Plate 1 x 2 with 1 Stud | Yellow |
| 1 | 6215.dat | Brick 2 x 3 with Curved Top | Yellow |
| 2 | 3622.dat | Brick 1 x 3 | Yellow |
| 2 | 3623.dat | Plate 1 x 3 | Yellow |
| 3 | 3710.dat | Plate 1 x 4 | Yellow |
| 1 | 44728.dat | Bracket 1 x 2 - 2 x 2 | Yellow |
| 4 | 3020.dat | Plate 2 x 4 | Yellow |
| 2 | 2357.dat | Brick 2 x 2 Corner | Yellow |
| 2 | 3037.dat | Slope Brick 45 2 x 4 | Yellow |
| 9 | 3023.dat | Plate 1 x 2 | Yellow |
| 1 | 3660.dat | Slope Brick 45 2 x 2 Inverted | Yellow |
| 6 | 3024.dat | Plate 1 x 1 | Yellow |
| 2 | 6541.dat | Technic Brick 1 x 1 with Hole | Yellow |
| 2 | 3747b.dat | Slope Brick 33 3 x 2 Inverted with Ribs between Studs | White |
| 2 | 32064b.dat | Technic Brick 1 x 2 with Axlehole Type 2 | White |
| 2 | 3665.dat | Slope Brick 45 2 x 1 Inverted | White |
| 2 | 3069b.dat | Tile 1 x 2 with Groove | White |
| 2 | 6636.dat | Tile 1 x 6 | White |
| 4 | 3001.dat | Brick 2 x 4 | White |
| 2 | 2420.dat | Plate 2 x 2 Corner | White |
| 4 | 2436.dat | Bracket 1 x 2 - 1 x 4 | White |
| 1 | 3003.dat | Brick 2 x 2 | White |
| 4 | 3040b.dat | Slope Brick 45 2 x 1 | White |
| 6 | 3004.dat | Brick 1 x 2 | White |
| 1 | 3894.dat | Technic Brick 1 x 6 with Holes | White |
| 4 | 3068b.dat | Tile 2 x 2 with Groove | White |
| 2 | 3794.dat | Plate 1 x 2 with 1 Stud | White |
| 2 | 3622.dat | Brick 1 x 3 | White |
| 4 | 3298.dat | Slope Brick 33 3 x 2 | White |
| 3 | 3034.dat | Plate 2 x 8 | White |
| 4 | 44728.dat | Bracket 1 x 2 - 2 x 2 | White |
| 8 | 3020.dat | Plate 2 x 4 | White |
| 6 | 3021.dat | Plate 2 x 3 | White |
| 2 | 3022.dat | Plate 2 x 2 | White |
| 2 | 3700.dat | Technic Brick 1 x 2 with Hole | White |
| 2 | 3023.dat | Plate 1 x 2 | White |
| 6 | 3660.dat | Slope Brick 45 2 x 2 Inverted | White |
| 4 | 3039.dat | Slope Brick 45 2 x 2 | White |
| 2 | 3010.dat | Brick 1 x 4 | White |

# Head and Neck

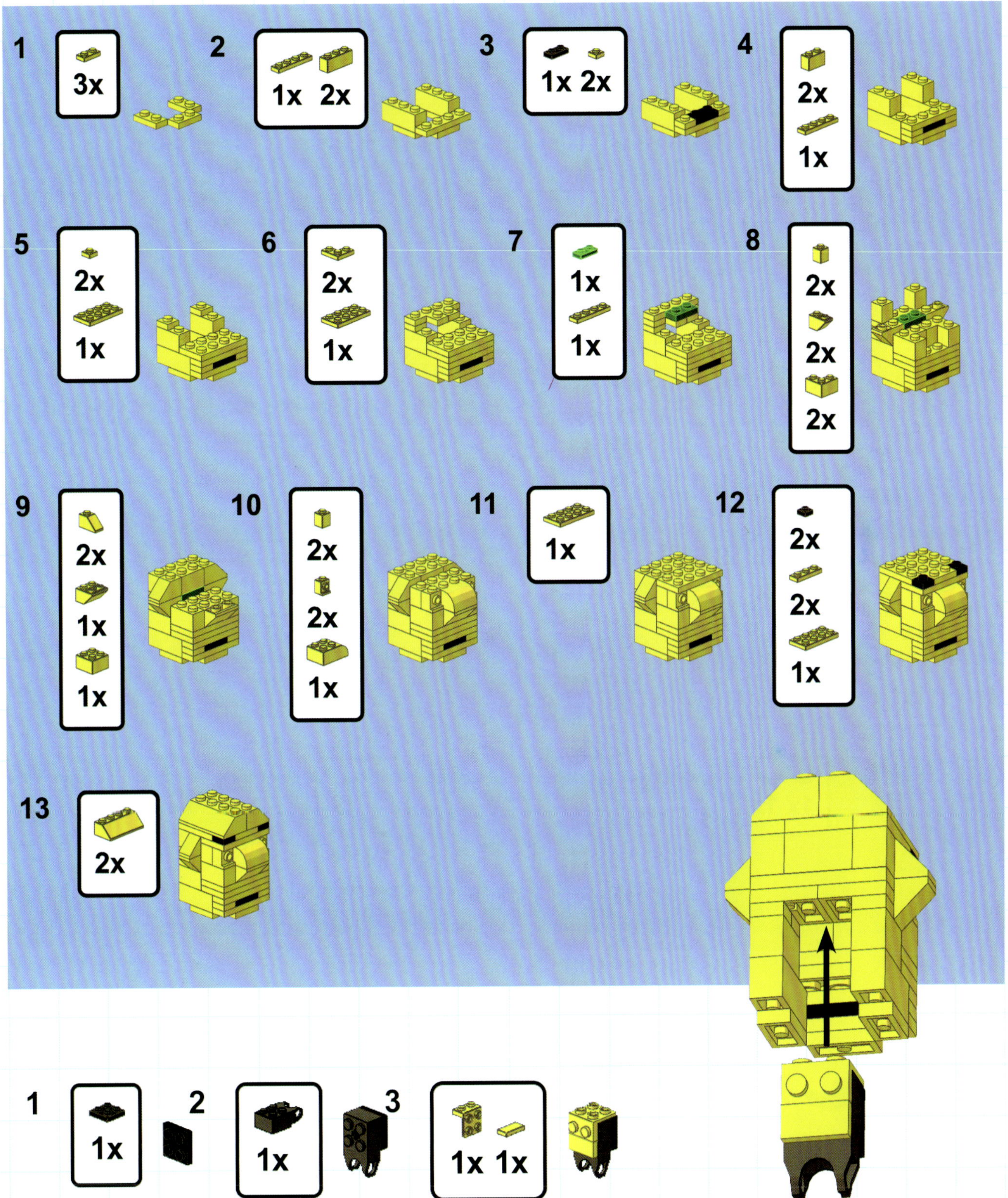

# Torso

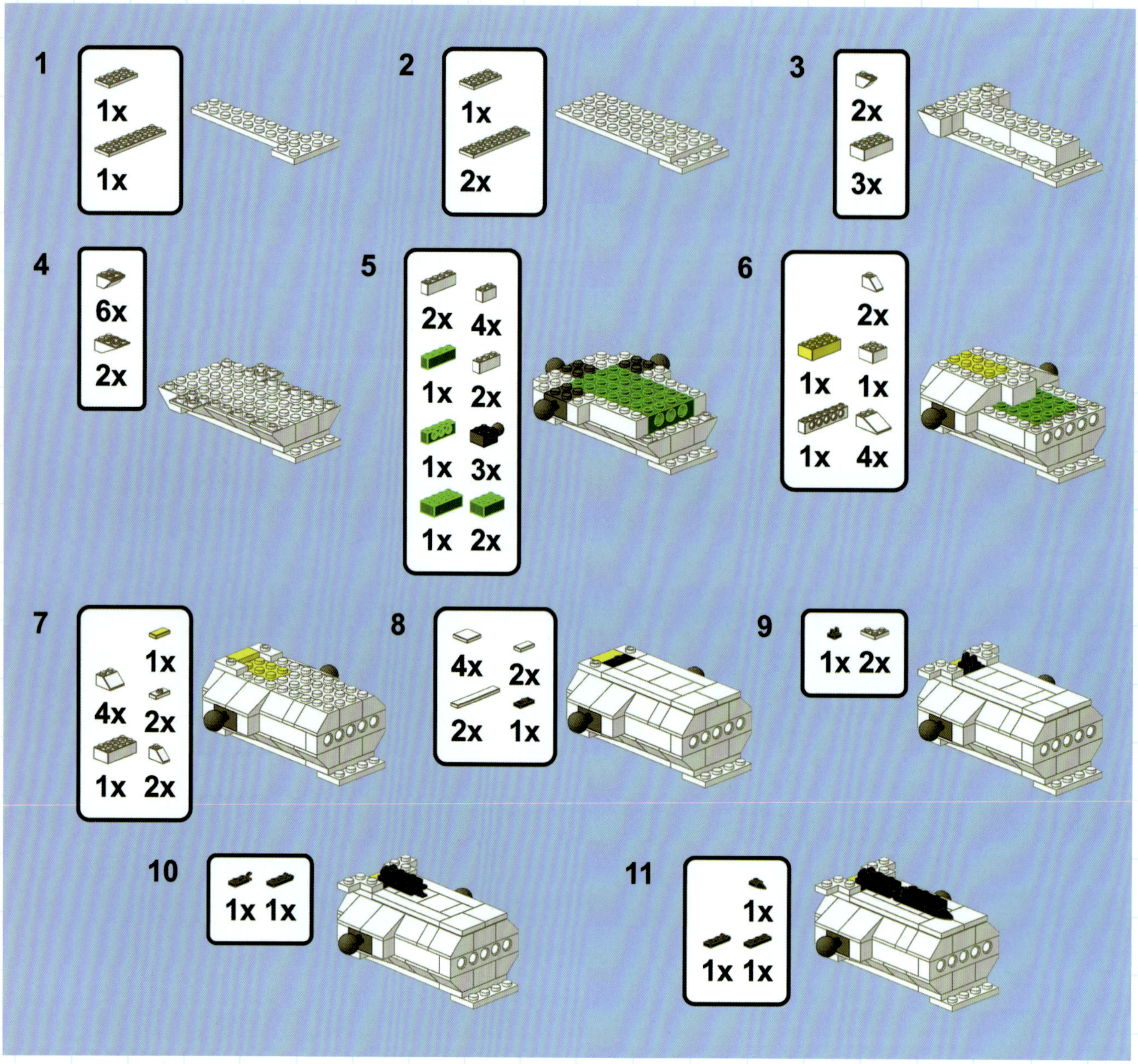

1
1x
1x
2
1x
2x
3
2x
3x
4
6x
2x
5
2x 4x
1x 2x
1x 3x
1x 2x
6
2x
1x 1x
1x 4x
7
1x
4x 2x
1x 2x
8
4x 2x
2x 1x
9
1x 2x
10
1x 1x
11
1x
1x 1x

# Waist

1
1x
2
2x
1x
3
2x
4
1x
5
2x
1x
6
2x
1x
7
2x
2x
8
1x

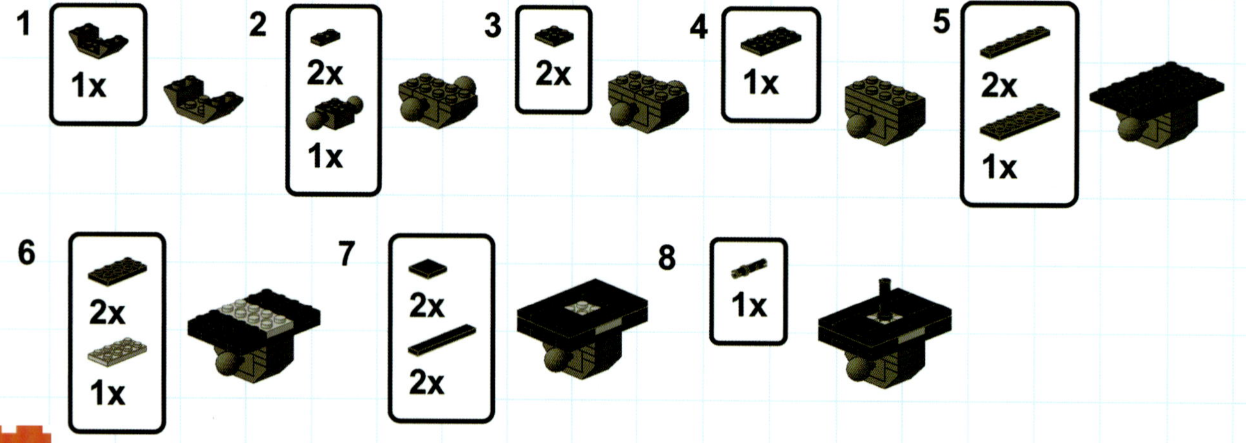

# Right Leg

### Upper

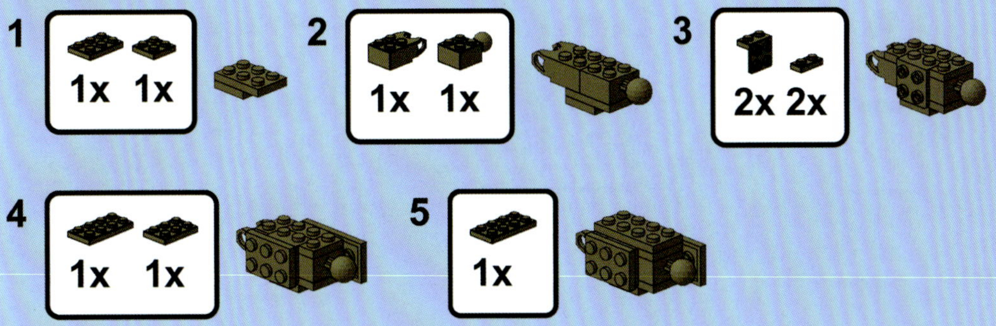

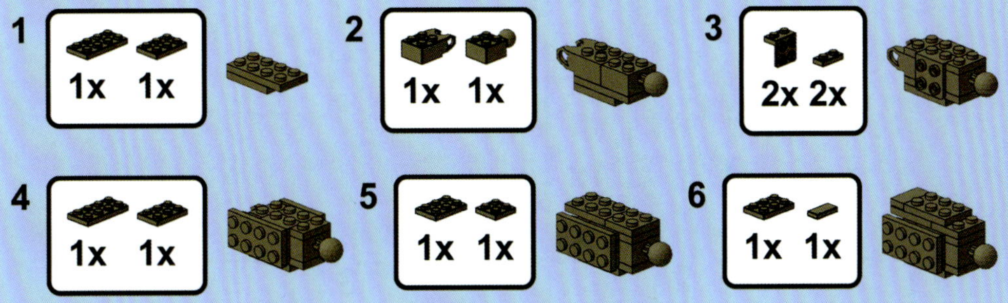

1
1x 1x
2
1x 1x
3
2x 2x
4
1x 1x
5
1x


### Lower

1
1x 1x
2
1x 1x
3
2x 2x
4
1x 1x
5
1x 1x
6
1x 1x


# Left Leg

### Upper

1
1x 1x
2
1x 1x
3
2x 2x
4
1x 1x
5
1x


### Lower

1
1x 1x
2
1x 1x
3
2x 2x
4
1x 1x
5
1x 1x
6
1x 1x

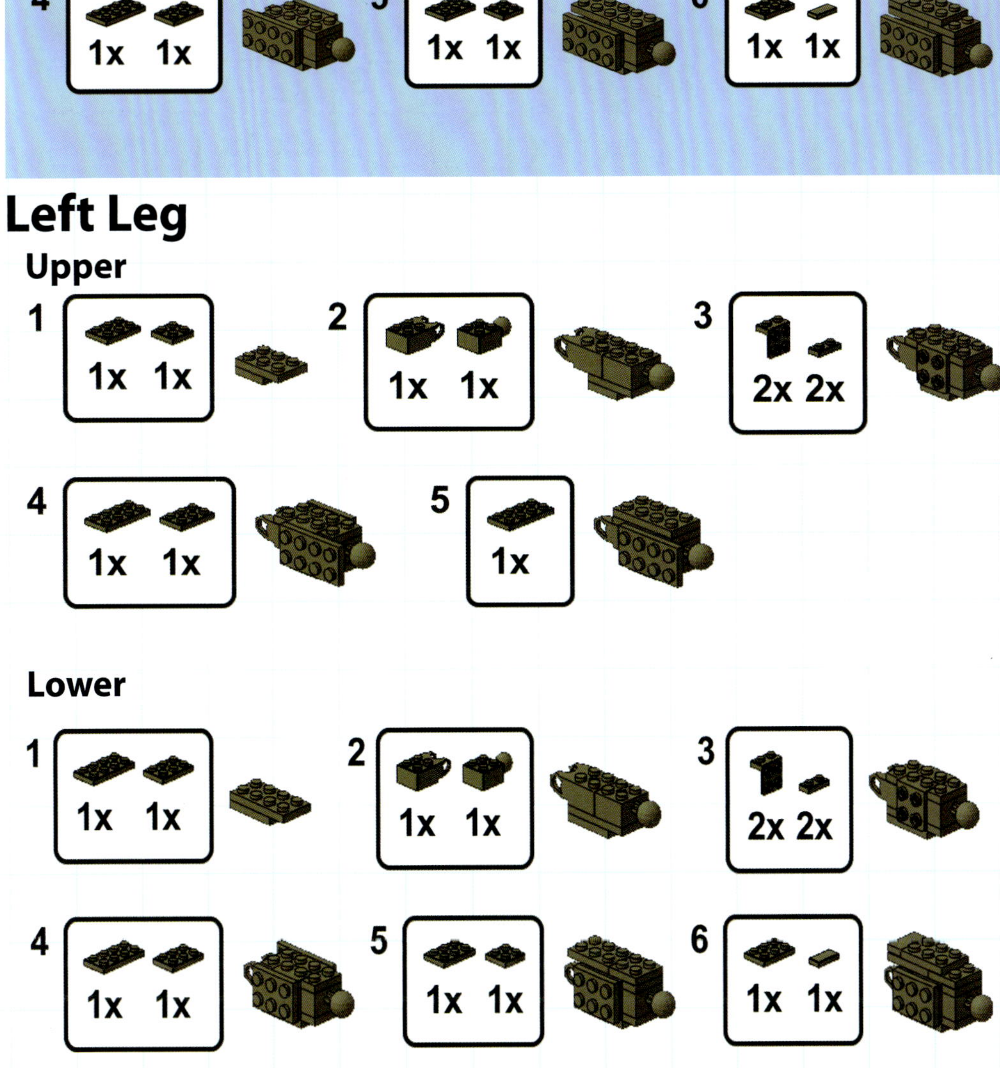

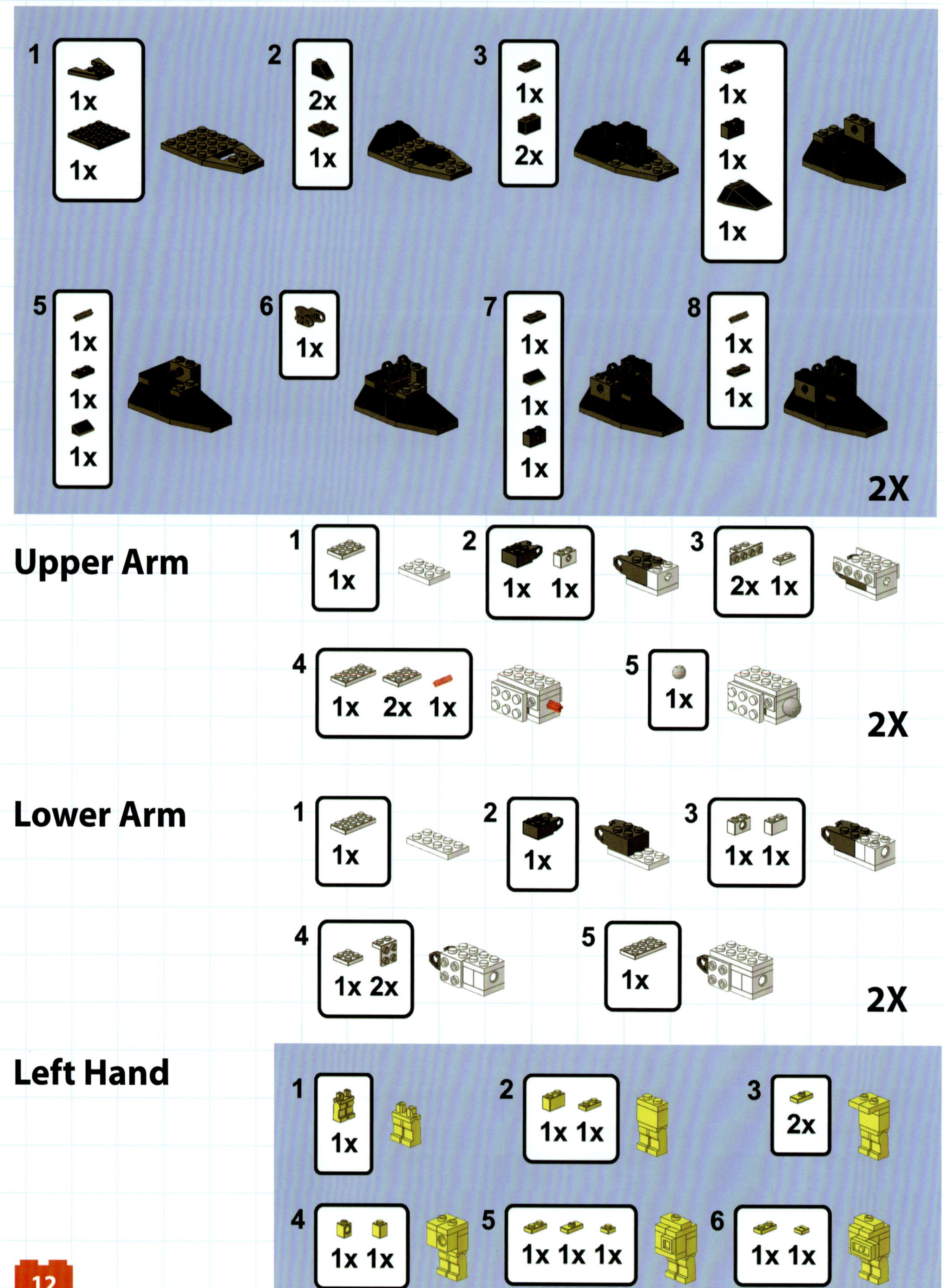
Feet
1 1x 1x
2 2x 1x
3 1x 2x
4 1x 1x 1x
5 1x 1x 1x
6 1x
7 1x 1x 1x
8 1x 1x
2X
Upper Arm
1 1x
2 1x 1x
3 2x 1x
4 1x 2x 1x
5 1x
2X
Lower Arm
1 1x
2 1x
3 1x 1x
4 1x 2x
5 1x
2X
Left Hand
1 1x
2 1x 1x
3 2x
4 1x 1x
5 1x 1x 1x
6 1x 1x

# Right Hand

1
1x
2
1x 1x
3
2x
4
1x 1x
5
1x 1x 1x
6
1x 1x


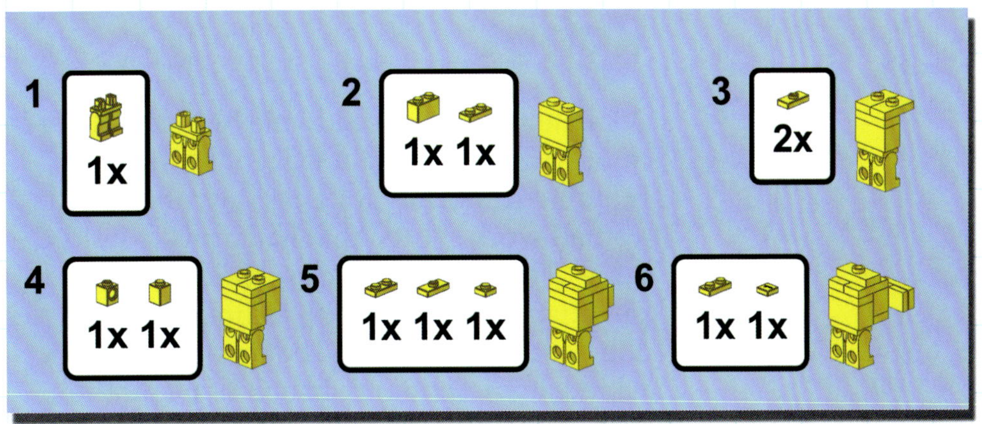

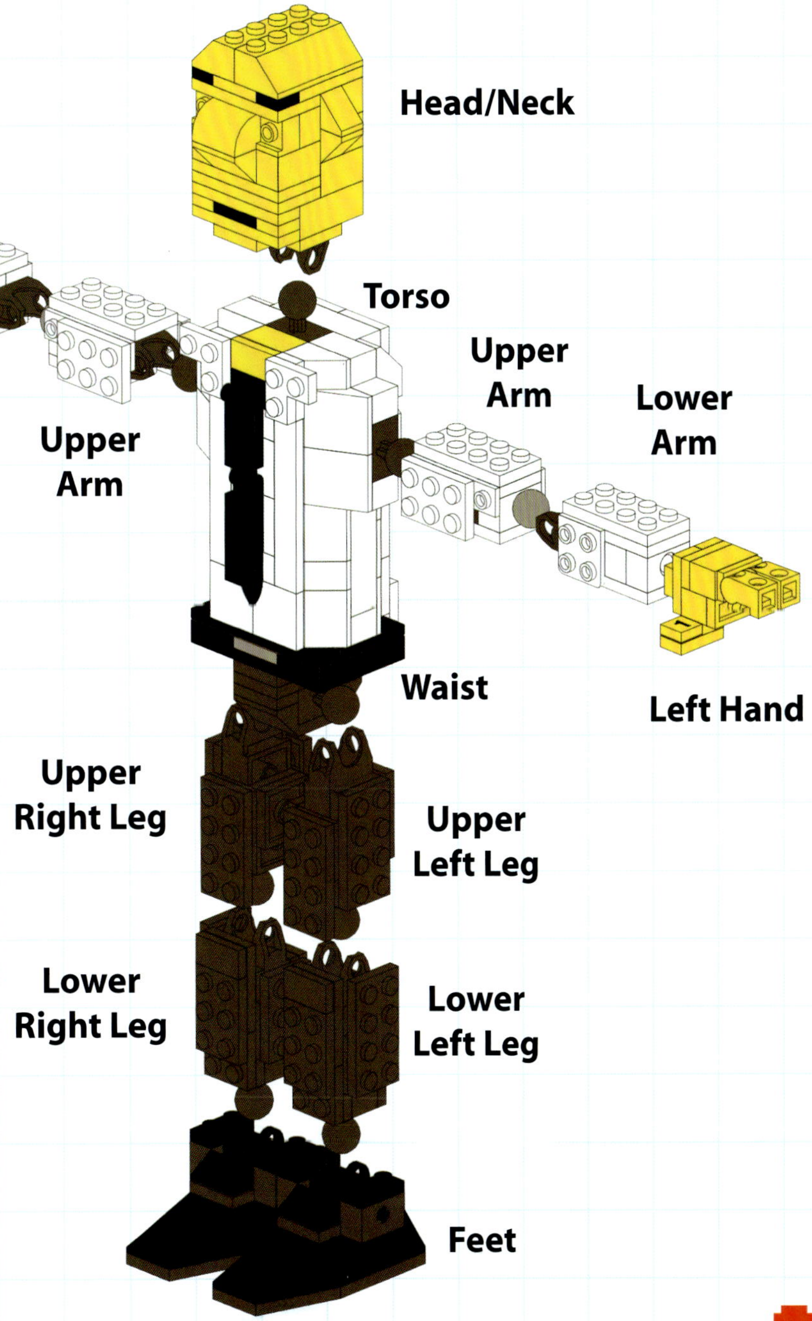

Head/Neck
Right Hand
Torso
Lower Arm
Upper Arm
Upper Arm
Lower Arm
Waist
Left Hand
Upper Right Leg
Upper Left Leg
Lower Right Leg
Lower Left Leg
Feet

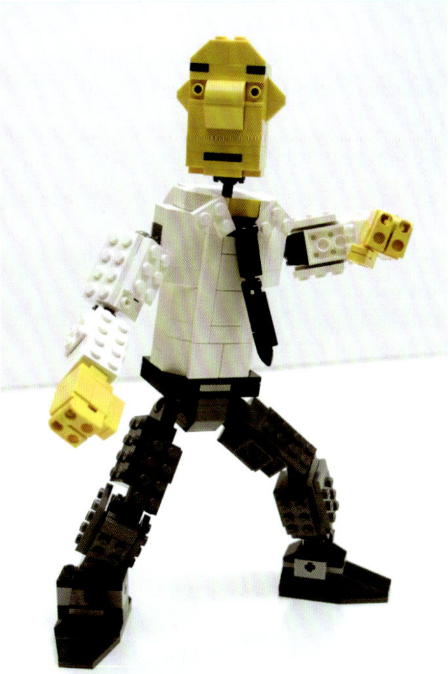

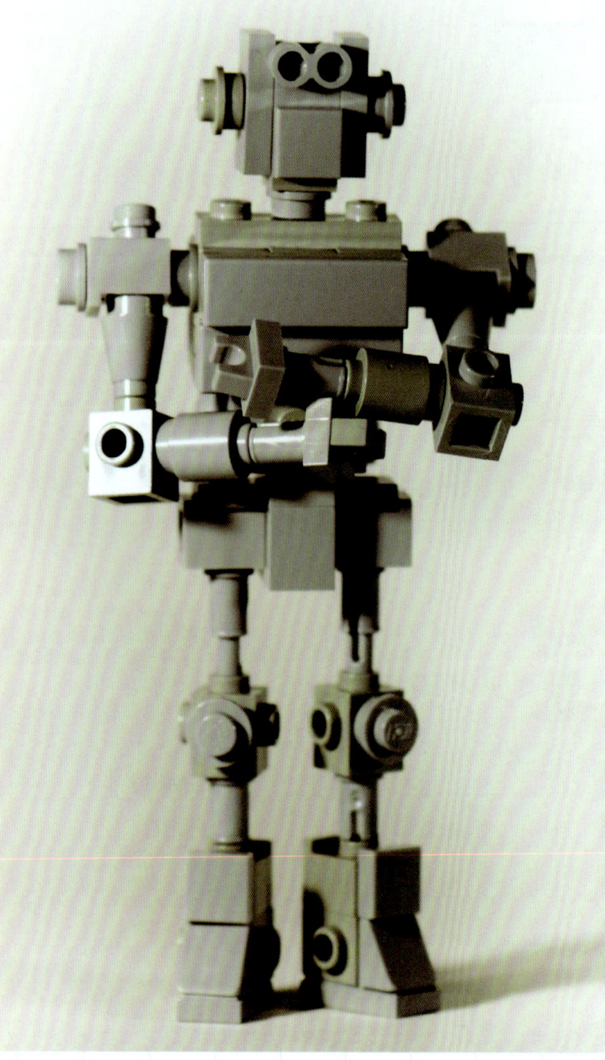

# Robot

A challenge was posed to me by a friend of mine to build a robot. I was in the midst of building frantically for a display, and I built a small work shuttle that had arms to hold items. The arms were made from a newer long pin attached to a tile with a clip on it (Take a look at the arms of the bot to the left to see what I am describing). In a fit of inspiration, that arm became the basis for the limbs of the robot. To make him cute, I built a head with eyes and ears - at this scale, a mouth would be tough to do.

The end result is articulated at the shoulders and hips, and the arms and legs can be positioned to 'bend.' You can make him as is, or change his color. See what you can add to him to make him your robot!

## Parts List

| Qty | Part | Description | Color |
|---|---|---|---|
| 2 | 2555.dat | Tile 1 x 1 with Clip | Light Bluish Gray |
| 1 | 3021.dat | Plate 2 x 3 | Light Bluish Gray |
| 2 | 3023.dat | Plate 1 x 2 | Light Bluish Gray |
| 1 | 3024.dat | Plate 1 x 1 | Light Bluish Gray |
| 6 | 3062b.dat | Brick 1 x 1 Round with Hollow Stud | Light Bluish Gray |
| 2 | 3069b.dat | Tile 1 x 2 with Groove | Light Bluish Gray |
| 6 | 3623.dat | Plate 1 x 3 | Light Bluish Gray |
| 2 | 3700.dat | Technic Brick 1 x 2 with Hole | Light Bluish Gray |
| 3 | 3794b.dat | Plate 1 x 2 with Groove with 1 Centre Stud | Light Bluish Gray |
| 8 | 4070.dat | Brick 1 x 1 with Headlight | Light Bluish Gray |
| 1 | 4274.dat | Technic Pin 1/2 | Blue |
| 7 | 4733.dat | Brick 1 x 1 with Studs on Four Sides | Light Bluish Gray |
| 10 | 6141.dat | Plate 1 x 1 Round | Light Bluish Gray |
| 4 | 6188.dat | Cone 1 x 1 | Light Bluish Gray |
| 2 | 6541.dat | Technic Brick 1 x 1 with Hole | Light Bluish Gray |
| 5 | 30039.dat | Tile 1 x 1 with Groove | Light Bluish Gray |
| 1 | 30162.dat | Minifig Tool Binoculars Town | Light Bluish Gray |
| 1 | 47905.dat | Brick 1 x 1 with Studs on Two Opposite Sides | Light Bluish Gray |
| 2 | 54200.dat | Slope Brick 31 1 x 1 x 2/3 | Light Bluish Gray |
| 8 | 61184.dat | Technic Pin 1/2 with Bar 2L | Light Bluish Gray |
| 3 | 63864.dat | Tile 1 x 3 with Groove | Light Bluish Gray |

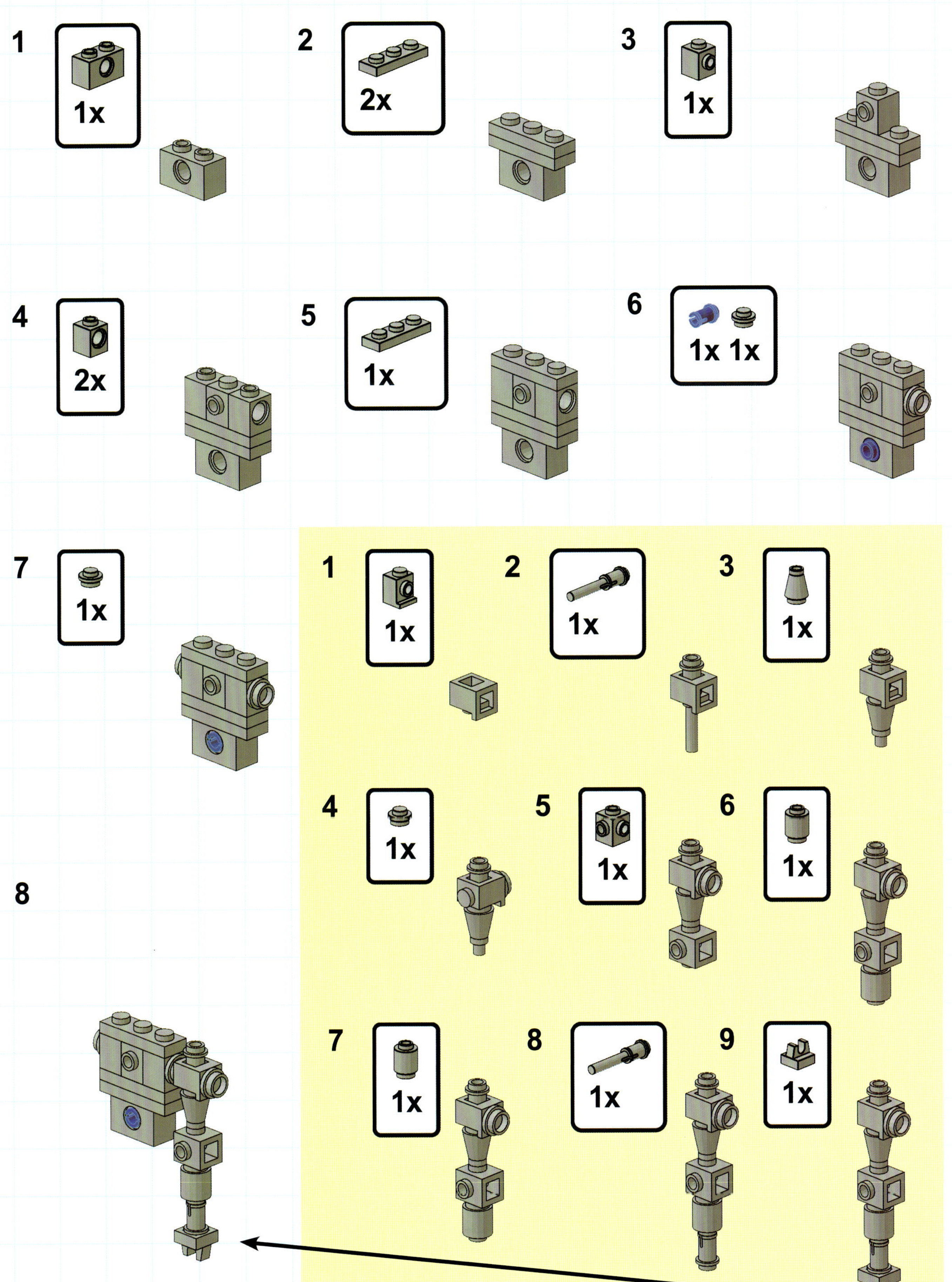
1
1x
2
2x
3
1x
4
2x
5
1x
6
1x 1x
7
1x
8
1
1x
2
1x
3
1x
4
1x
5
1x
6
1x
7
1x
8
1x
9
1x

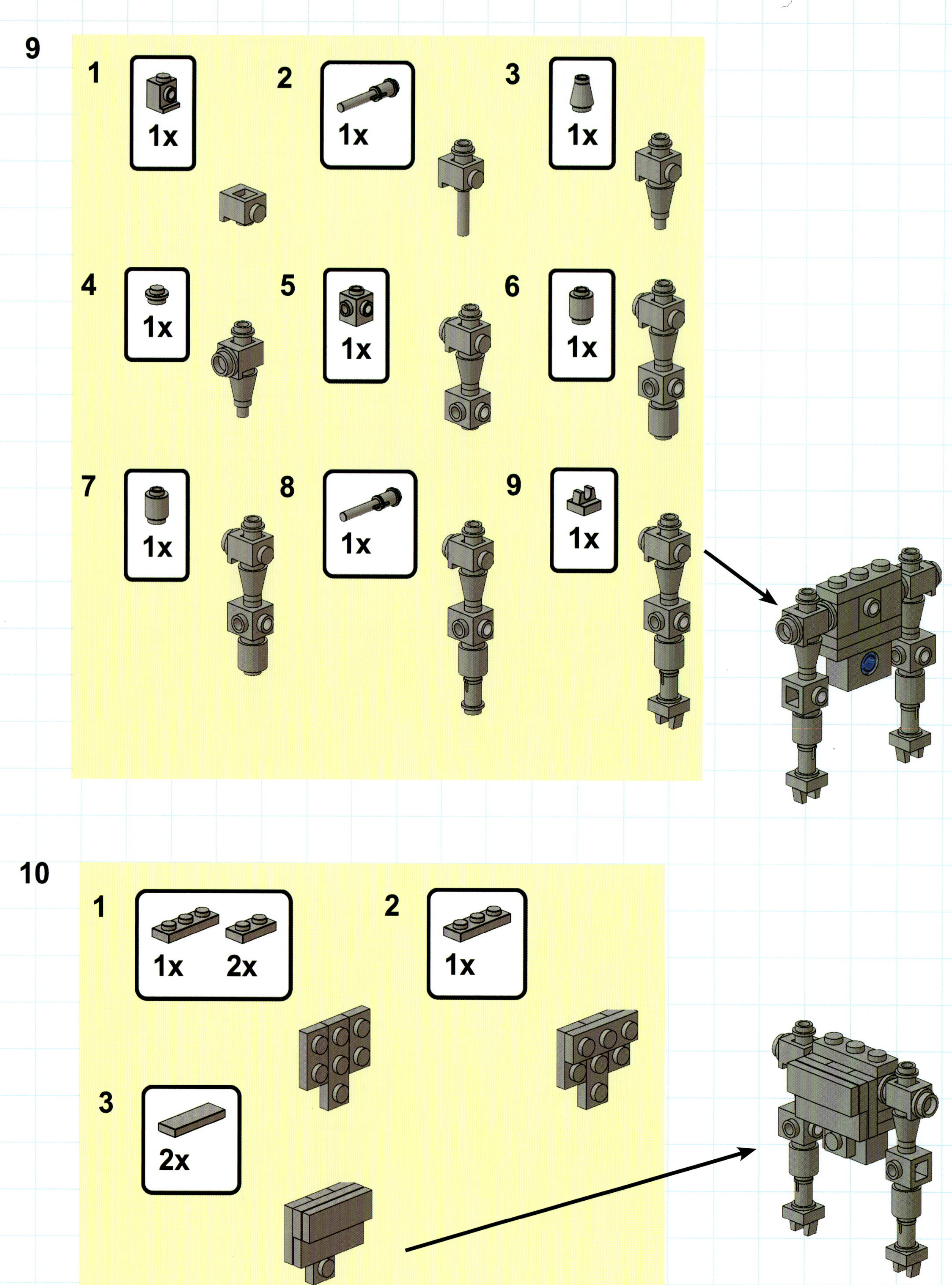
9
1
1x
2
1x
3
1x
4
1x
5
1x
6
1x
7
1x
8
1x
9
1x
10
1
1x
2x
2
1x
3
2x

11
1
1x
2
1x
1x
1x
3
2x
4
2x
5
2x

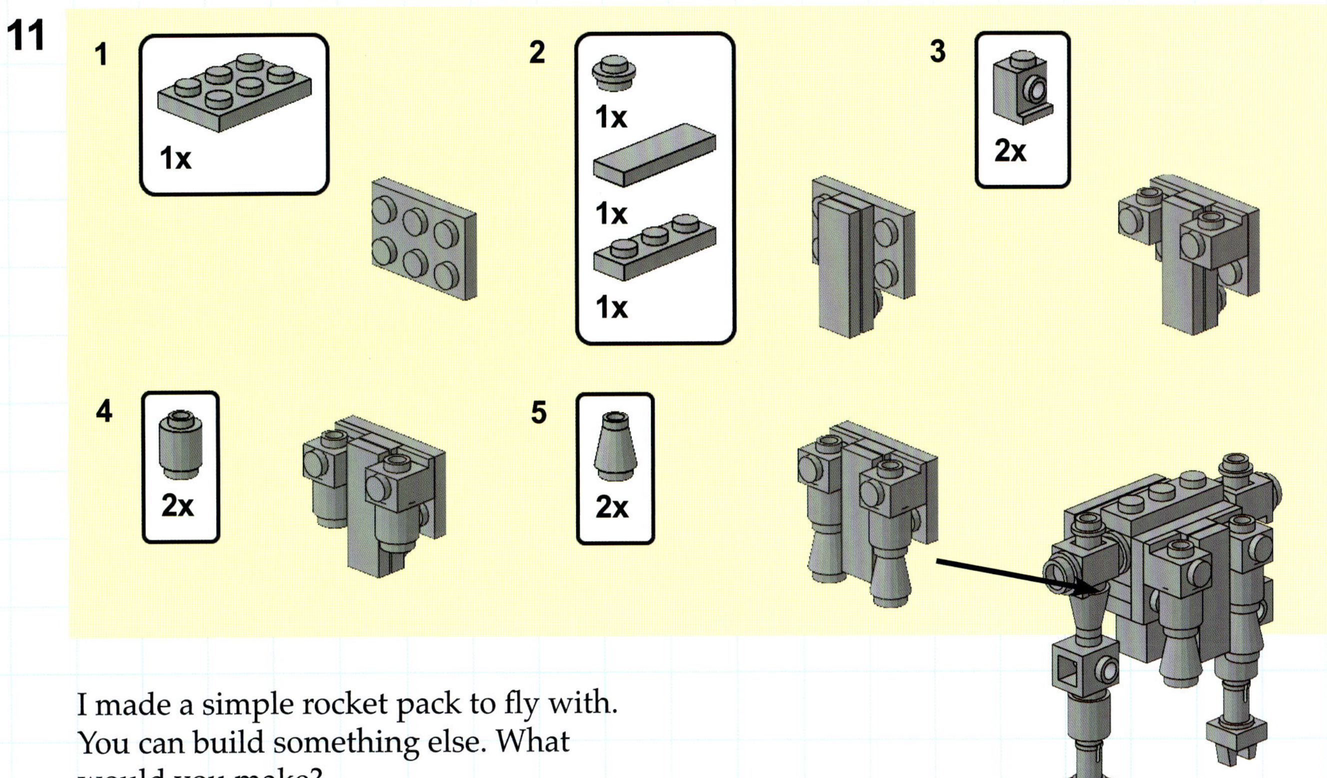

I made a simple rocket pack to fly with. You can build something else. What would you make?

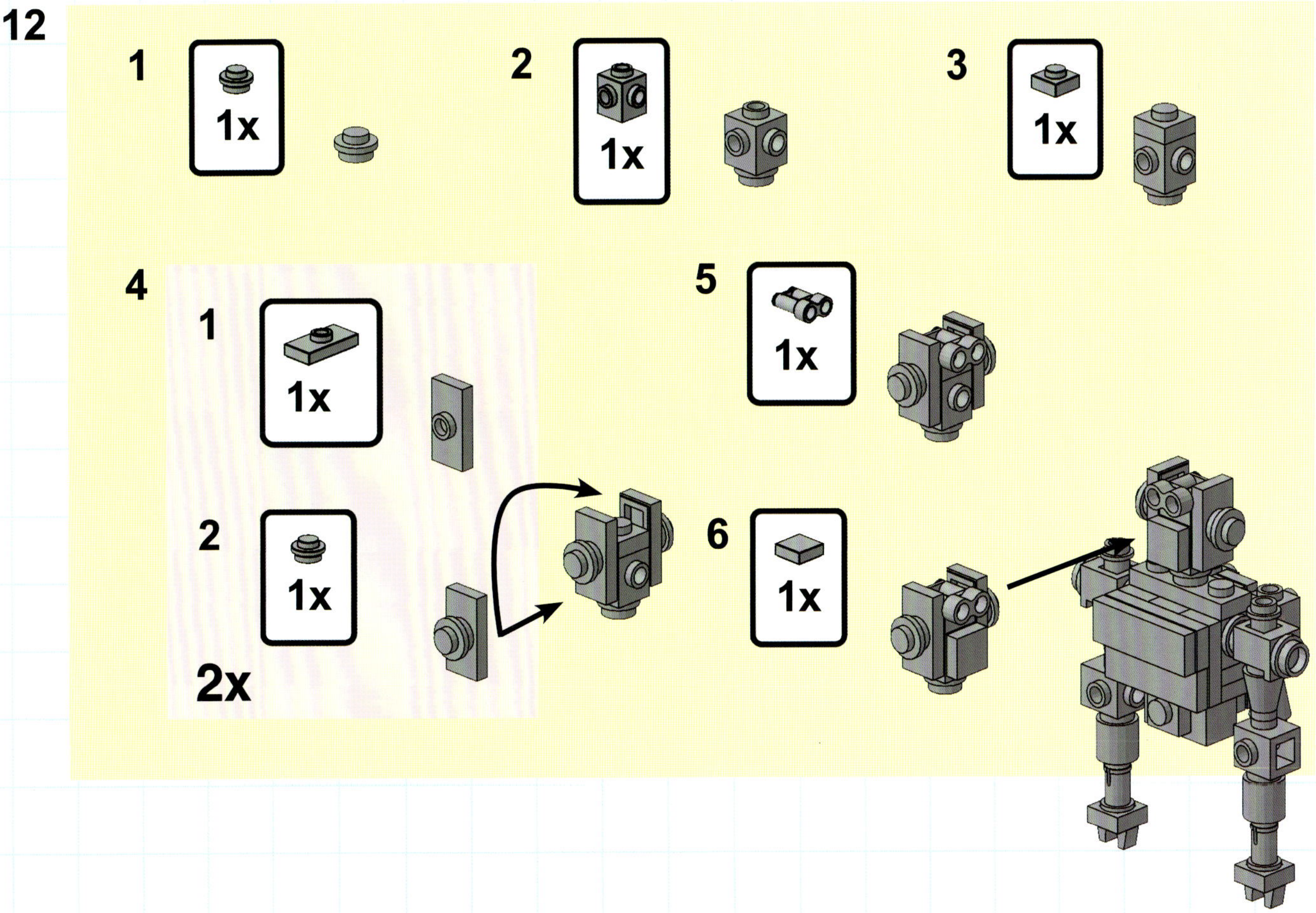

12
1
1x
2
1x
3
1x
4
1
1x
2
1x
2x
5
1x
6
1x

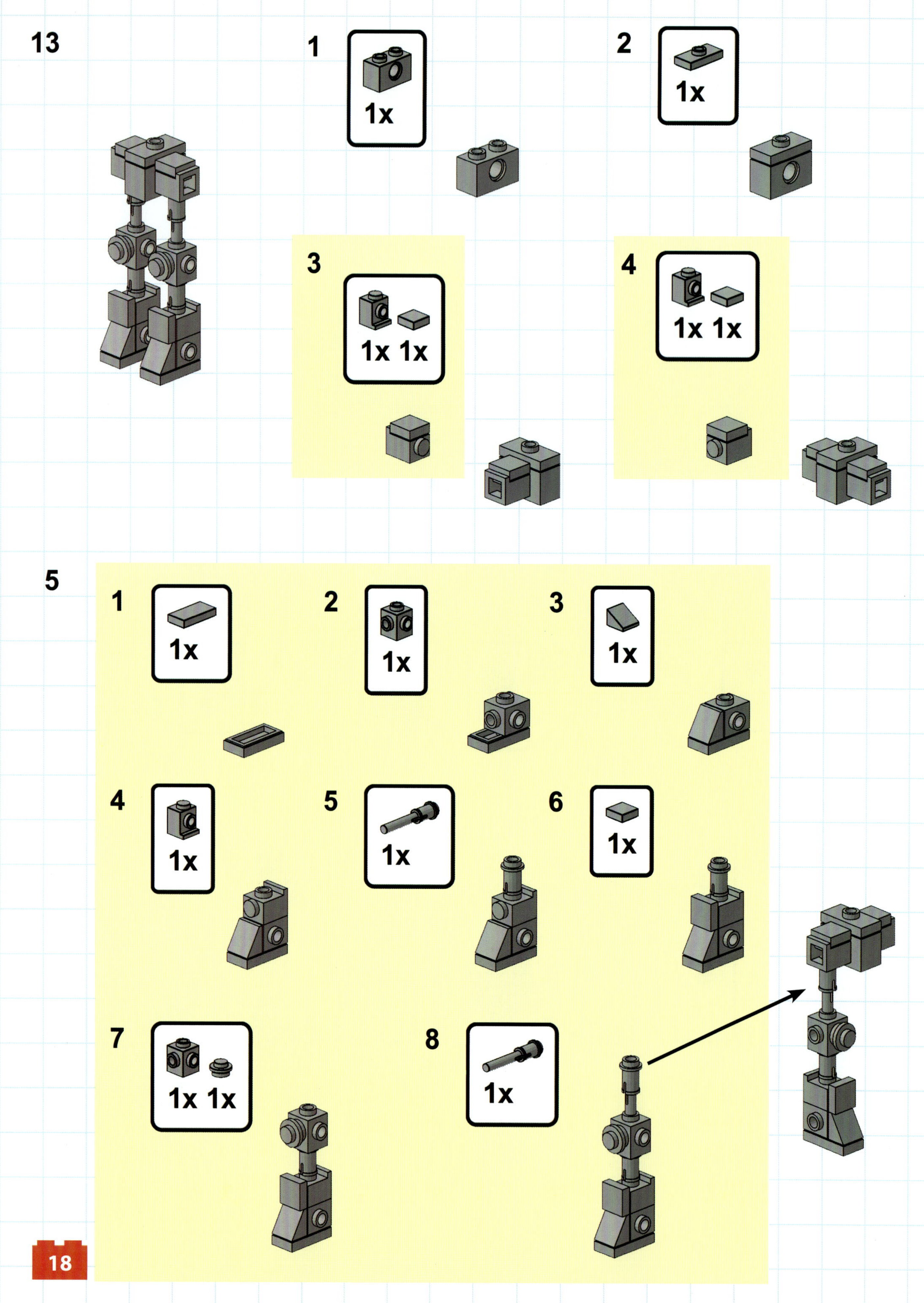

13
1
1x
2
1x
3
1x 1x
4
1x 1x
5
1
1x
2
1x
3
1x
4
1x
5
1x
6
1x
7
1x 1x
8
1x

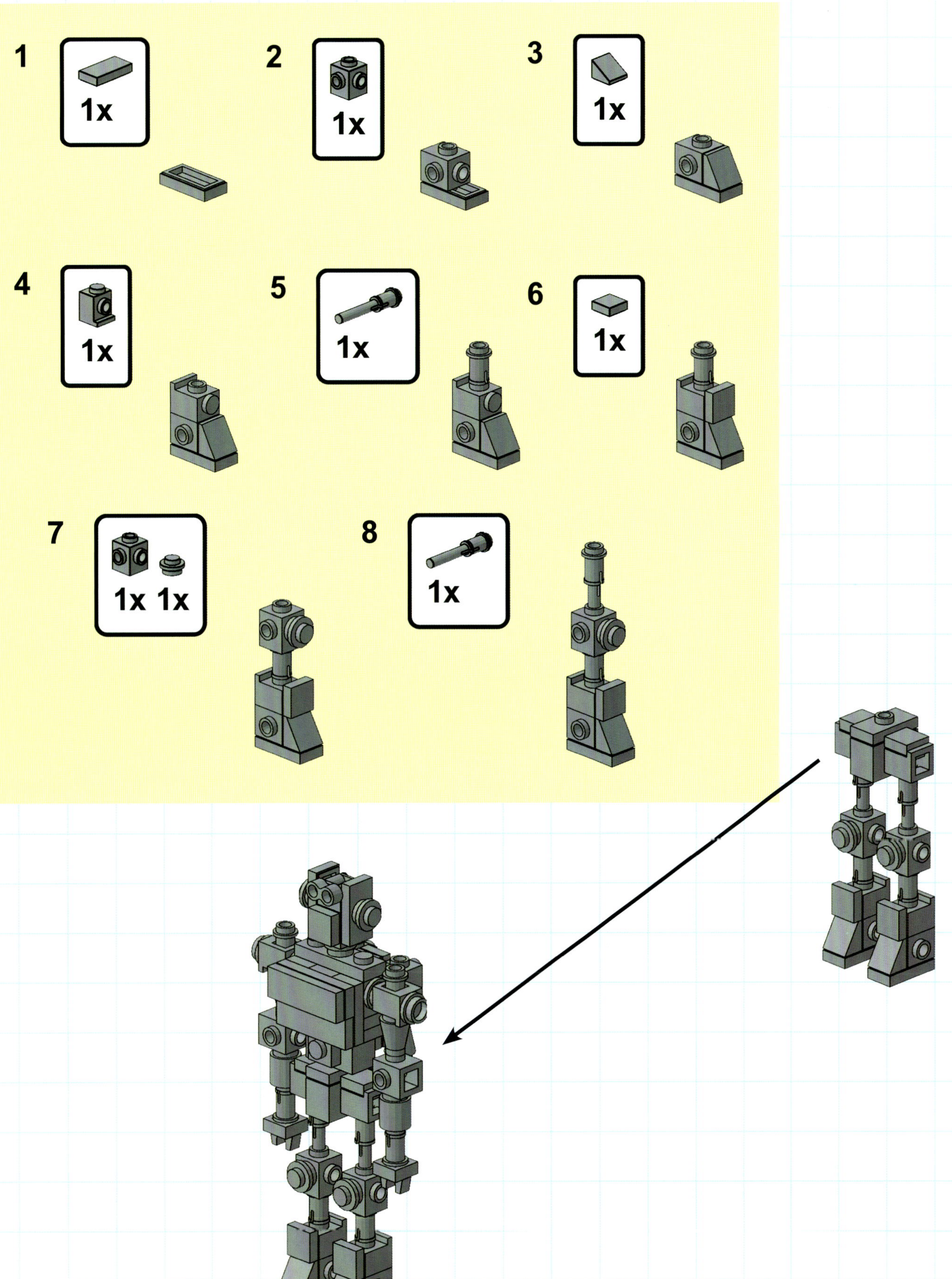
1
1x
2
1x
3
1x
4
1x
5
1x
6
1x
7
1x 1x
8
1x

*This article and model first appeared in Issue 10 of* BrickJournal.

*Mike Huffman's first puzzle.*

*Photograph by Mike Huffman*

# Puzzling LEGO® Models:

## Building the World's Smallest LEGO Sliding Puzzle

*Article and Photography by John Cooper*

One of the best parts of being an Adult Fan Of LEGO (AFOL) is the wonderful collaboration and inspiration that occurs within the AFOL community. Here's a good example of how one builder's creative idea became the inspiration for another builder to push the concept to the next level.

Back in November 2006, Mike Huffman was inspired by the LEGO Mosaic sets (#6162 and #6163) and built a fun sliding puzzle. Mike shared his creation with a post on LUGNET (www.lugnet.com, post is http://news.lugnet.com/announce/moc/?n=3647), along with some linked photos online. The genius of his design was the interlocking rail and groove sliding modules. Many people have built simple non-interlocking sliding puzzles out of LEGO, but this was the first interlocking design I had seen. Immediately I set out to build my own puzzle to fill a 32x32 stud baseplate.

Mike's puzzle design used a 6x6 stud sized sliding module. After building my initial puzzle, I thought it would be great to have a smaller module, allowing more sliding pieces in a similar-sized puzzle. After many attempts with overly complicated 4x4 stud designs, I found a simple solution.

Around this time I got in a dialog with Tommy Armstrong (www.brickengraver.com) about some projects using engraved and printed LEGO tiles. Tommy laid down the challenge "What's the smallest size sliding puzzle you can make?" I began more experimentation with ideas for building an even smaller sliding module. As is often the case, the best solution was based on clever simplicity. An effective 2x2 stud sliding module was devised using an upside down tile.

The puzzle frames utilize the same slotted bricks and rail plates from Mike's original design. Since slotted bricks are only available in 1x4 size, it takes a little creativity in designing the frame for smaller puzzles, particularly the corners. But otherwise, any size puzzle can be made in two stud increments.

One thing that has always annoyed me about sliding puzzles is the empty space necessary to allow movement of the pieces. I wanted to display my LEGO puzzles when not in use, so I made a removable filler piece for display. That way there isn't an empty spot, and the filler piece drops out by turning the puzzle over and tapping it gently.

Mike's original sliding puzzle used 1x1 bricks to create the puzzle picture. With the smaller puzzles it's difficult to get a recognizable image with the resolution of the 1x1 bricks. This is where Tommy's expertise shines. Engraved or printed tiles are the perfect medium for a detailed image in a small puzzle. When the Nintendo DS Lite armor cases were released in late 2009 with LEGO Star Wars and Indiana Jones images printed on tiles,

*Above: Some of John Cooper's puzzles.*
*Right: Mike's puzzle module design.*

naturally I had to build sliding puzzles in that size as well.

The final size reduction came as a suggestion from Gary McIntire. Gary reminded me about the new 2x2 jumper plate that was introduced in 2009. When the part was first released I considered it for use in the puzzles, but discounted the idea since the part was expensive and only available in game sets sold in Europe. But since then, the new part was showing up worldwide in new sets, so it was becoming more affordable. Gary also pointed out one benefit I hadn't considered--the engraved or printed tiles could be attached directly to the 2x2 jumper plates. This reduced the height of the puzzles by nearly 40 percent. While the 2x2 jumper plates don't slide quite as well as the 2x2 tiles, they certainly offer a significant size reduction.

So what is the world's smallest LEGO element interlocking sliding puzzle size? Obviously a non-interlocking sliding puzzle with 1x1 modules could be built, but it wouldn't survive the test of being turned upside down. An interlocking puzzle with just four modules can easily be made. But when the filler piece is removed, the remaining three pieces would slide around in order. I personally wouldn't consider this a puzzle, since no real thought is required to get the pieces back in order. So my vote would be that a six module LEGO element interlocking sliding puzzle is the world's smallest.

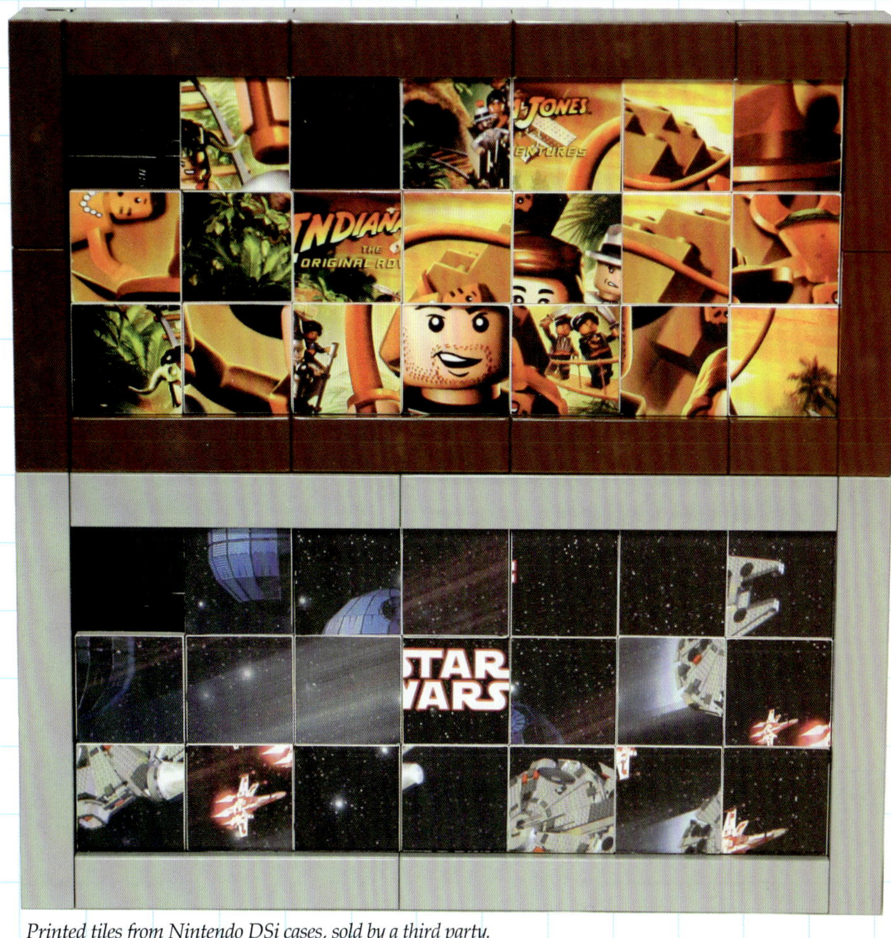


*Printed tiles from Nintendo DSi cases, sold by a third party.*

Of course I realize anytime you claim the "World's Smallest" title, someone else will come along with an even smaller design. But I see that as a continuation of the collaboration and inspiration process, so bring it on!

## The Evolution of a Puzzle Module
### or the Incredible Shrinking Piece!

Here's a look at how the puzzle module has decreased in size, from Mike Huffman's initial module at left to John Cooper's and Gary McIntire's latest iteration at right.

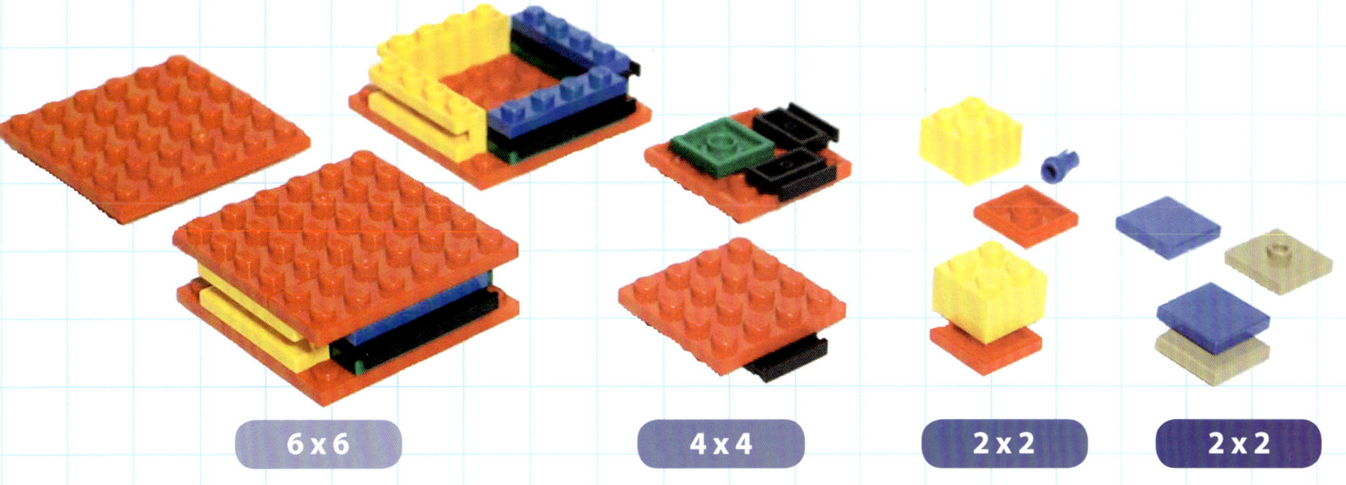

# Sliding LEGO® Puzzle:

## 9 -Module Puzzle

*Design by John Cooper*

Here are the instructions to make a 3 module by 3 module puzzle. This will create a puzzle with 8 sliding modules and 1 insert module. With some thought, this can be upsized to a 4 module by 4 module or larger. Also the colors of the frame can be changed if desired.

## Parts List

| Qty | Part | Description | Color |
|---|---|---|---|
| 1 | 3023.dat | Plate 1 x 2 | White |
| 9 | 4274.dat | Technic Pin 1/2 | White |
| 2 | 6636.dat | Tile 1 x 6 | Black |
| 5 | 32028.dat | Plate 1 x 2 with Door Rail | White |
| 2 | 3460.dat | Plate 1 x 8 | White |
| 9 | 3068b.dat | Tile 2 x 2 with Groove | Black |
| 17 | 3068b.dat | Tile 2 x 2 with Groove | White |
| 1 | 4865.dat | Panel 1 x 2 x 1 | White |
| 1 | 3070b.dat | Tile 1 x 1 with Groove | White |
| 2 | 3024.dat | Plate 1 x 1 | White |
| 2 | 3008.dat | Brick 1 x 8 | White |
| 1 | 41539.dat | Plate 8 x 8 | Black |
| 9 | 3003.dat | Brick 2 x 2 | White |
| 2 | 3009.dat | Brick 1 x 6 | White |
| 2 | 3666.dat | Plate 1 x 6 | White |
| 3 | 2653.dat | Brick 1 x 4 with Groove | White |
| 2 | 4162.dat | Tile 1 x 8 | Black |

1

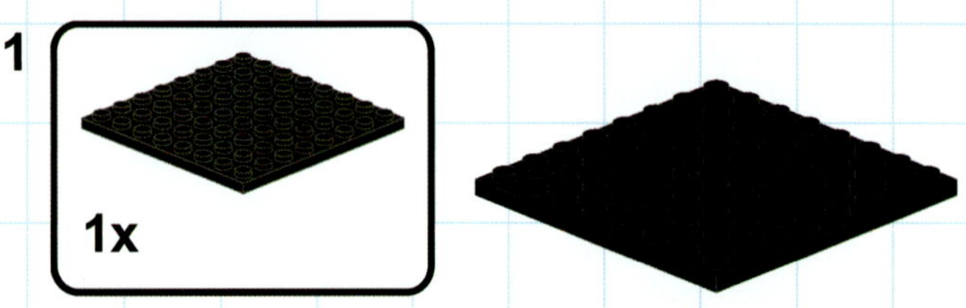


2

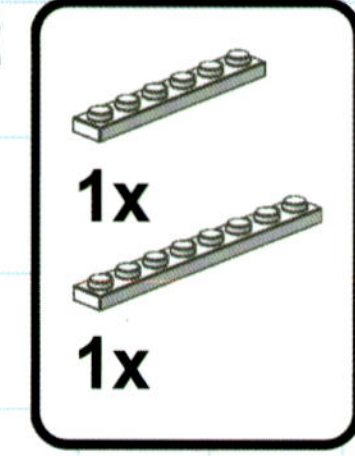


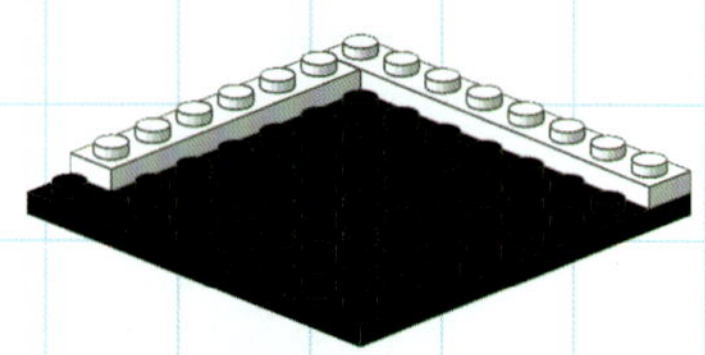

3

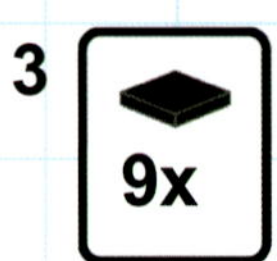


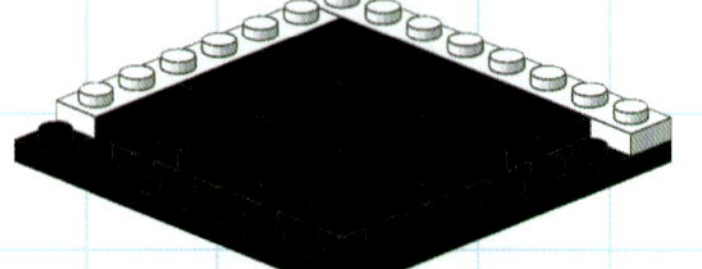

4

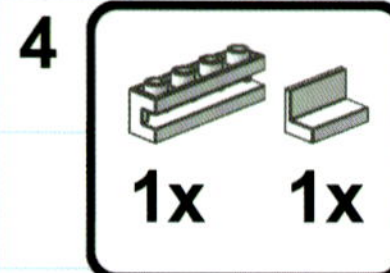


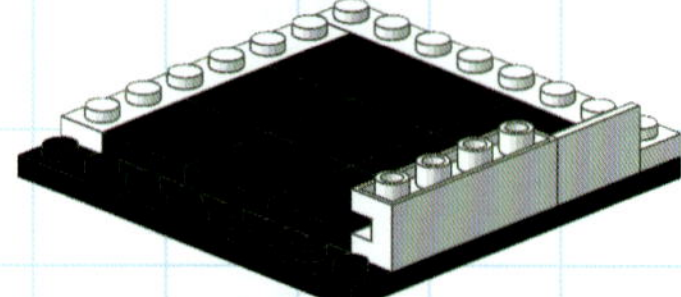

5

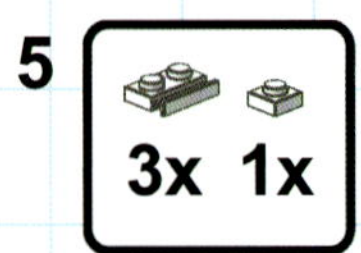


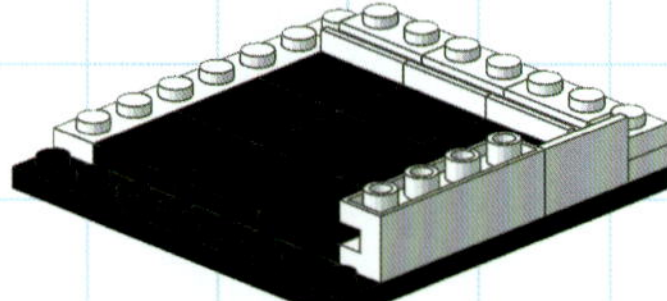

6

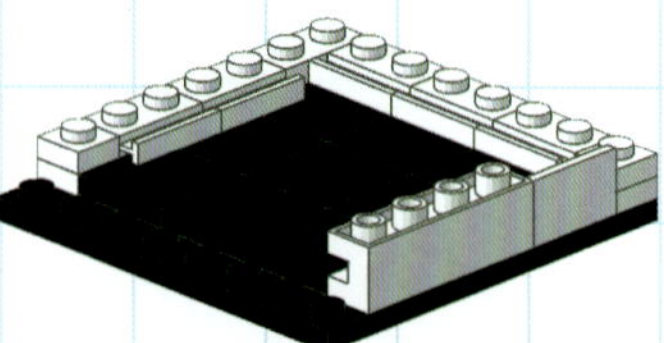

7

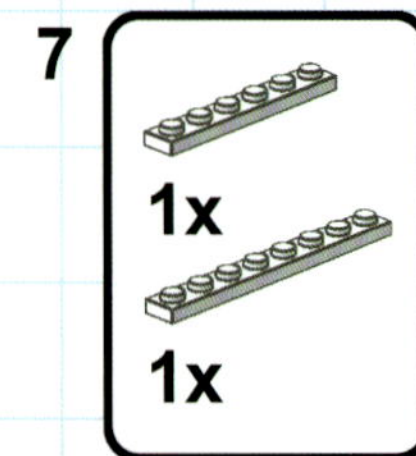


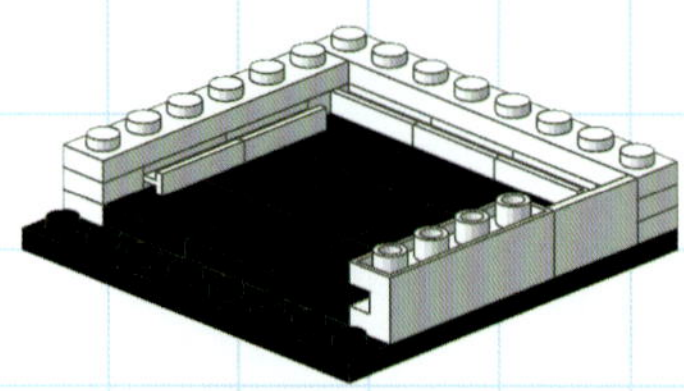

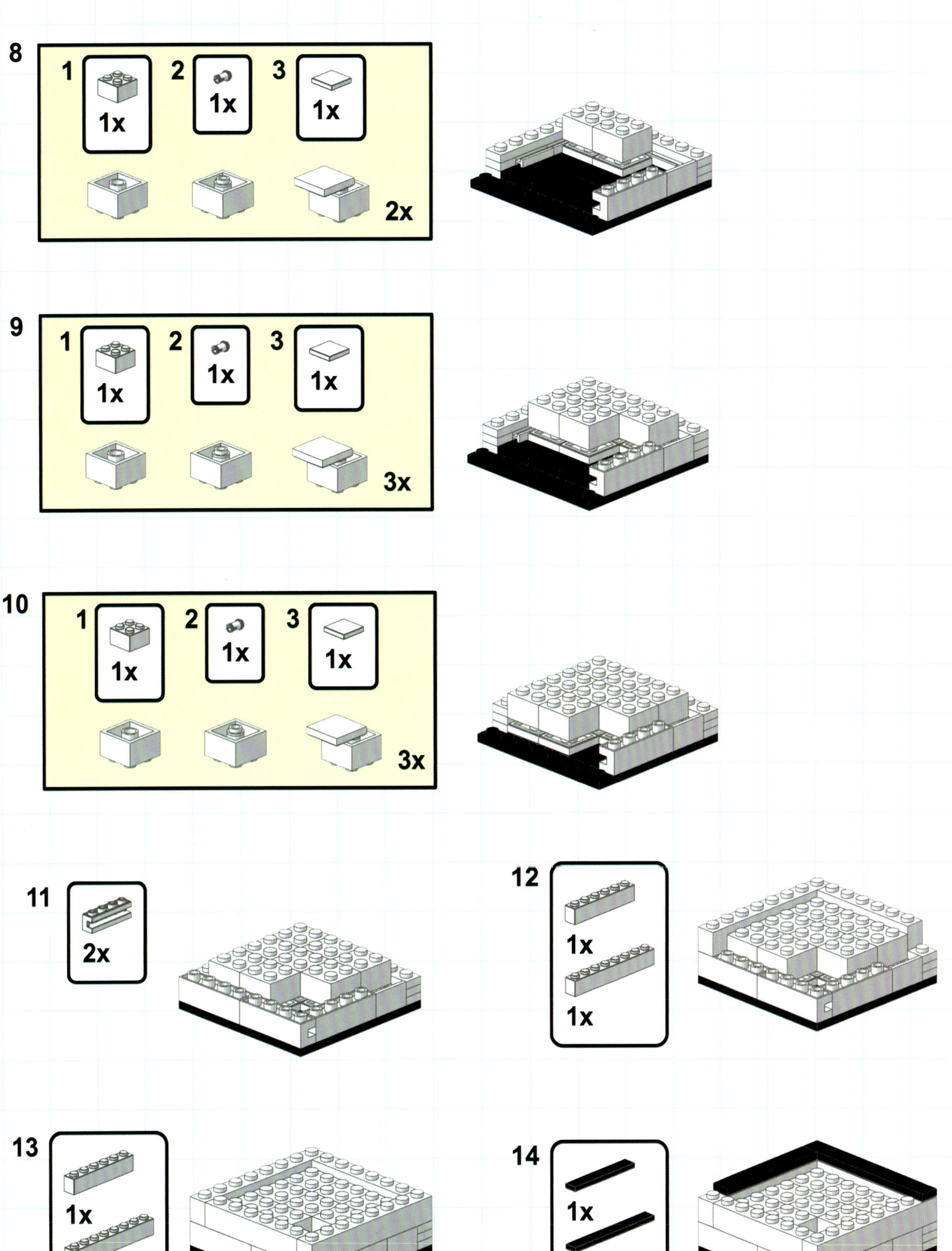
8
1
1x
2
1x
3
1x
2x
9
1
1x
2
1x
3
1x
3x
10
1
1x
2
1x
3
1x
3x
11
2x
12
1x
1x
13
1x
1x
14
1x
1x

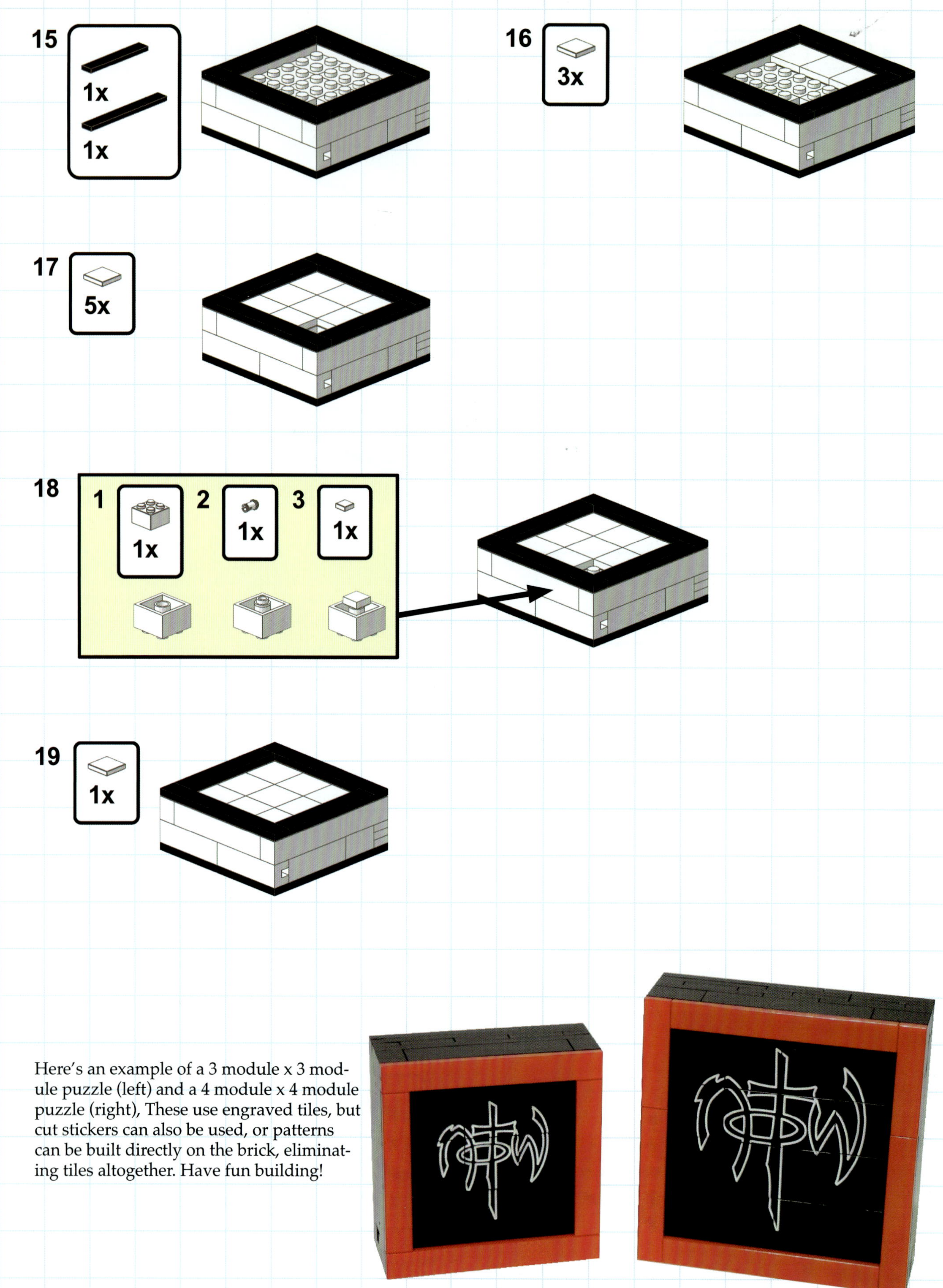


Here's an example of a 3 module x 3 module puzzle (left) and a 4 module x 4 module puzzle (right), These use engraved tiles, but cut stickers can also be used, or patterns can be built directly on the brick, eliminating tiles altogether. Have fun building!

# Heavy Duty Truck

## Minifigure Scale

*Model by Joe Meno*

This truck was built about ten years ago when I wanted to see how accurate I could build in minifigure scale. This is based on an Oshkosh Severe Load Vehicle, which is used by the military to deliver cargo. I downloaded some blueprints and matched them up to a minifgure compatible scale - I think I arbitrarily made the truck eight studs wide and worked from there.

The truck has a movable crane, the roof of the cab can be removed to place minifigures, and the doors open. Also the rear cargo area can be modified to have other containers, so you can build pallets or whatever you want.

## Parts List

| Qty | Part | Description | Color |
|---|---|---|---|
| 2 | 2357.dat | Brick 2 x 2 Corner | Light Bluish Gray |
| 2 | 2412b.dat | Tile 1 x 2 Grille with Groove | Dark Bluish Gray |
| 2 | 2429c01.dat | Hinge Plate 1 x 4 (Complete) | Black |
| 1 | 2431.dat | Tile 1 x 4 with Groove | Light Bluish Gray |
| 1 | 2431p52.dat | Tile 1 x 4 with Danger Stripes Black Pattern | Yellow |
| 2 | 2436b.dat | Bracket 1 x 2 - 1 x 4 Type 2 | Light Bluish Gray |
| 1 | 2445.dat | Plate 2 x 12 | Light Bluish Gray |
| 1 | 2452.dat | Hinge Plate 1 x 2 with 3 Fingers On Side | Black |
| 1 | 2458.dat | Brick 1 x 2 with Pin | Light Bluish Gray |
| 1 | 2540.dat | Plate 1 x 2 with Handle | Light Bluish Gray |
| 4 | 2654.dat | Dish 2 x 2 | Light Bluish Gray |
| 4 | 2877.dat | Brick 1 x 2 with Grille | Dark Bluish Gray |
| 17 | 3001.dat | Brick 2 x 4 | Light Bluish Gray |
| 3 | 3002.dat | Brick 2 x 3 | Light Bluish Gray |
| 2 | 3003.dat | Brick 2 x 2 | Light Bluish Gray |
| 2 | 3004.dat | Brick 1 x 2 | Light Bluish Gray |
| 2 | 3005.dat | Brick 1 x 1 | Dark Bluish Gray |

| Qty | Part | Description | Color |
|---|---|---|---|
| 2 | 3006.dat | Brick 2 x 10 | Light Bluish Gray |
| 4 | 3007.dat | Brick 2 x 8 | Light Bluish Gray |
| 1 | 3008.dat | Brick 1 x 8 | Light Bluish Gray |
| 6 | 3009.dat | Brick 1 x 6 | Light Bluish Gray |
| 1 | 3010.dat | Brick 1 x 4 | Light Bluish Gray |
| 1 | 3020.dat | Plate 2 x 4 | Dark Bluish Gray |
| 1 | 3020.dat | Plate 2 x 4 | Light Bluish Gray |
| 1 | 3021.dat | Plate 2 x 3 | Dark Bluish Gray |
| 2 | 3021.dat | Plate 2 x 3 | Light Bluish Gray |
| 3 | 3023.dat | Plate 1 x 2 | Light Bluish Gray |
| 3 | 3023.dat | Plate 1 x 2 | Black |
| 4 | 3024.dat | Plate 1 x 1 | Black |
| 1 | 3031.dat | Plate 4 x 4 | Dark Bluish Gray |
| 1 | 3034.dat | Plate 2 x 8 | Light Bluish Gray |
| 7 | 3036.dat | Plate 6 x 8 | Light Bluish Gray |
| 1 | 3039.dat | Slope Brick 45 2 x 2 | Dark Bluish Gray |
| 4 | 3039.dat | Slope Brick 45 2 x 2 | Light Bluish Gray |
| 6 | 3040b.dat | Slope Brick 45 2 x 1 | Light Bluish Gray |
| 8 | 3062b.dat | Brick 1 x 1 Round with Hollow Stud | Light Bluish Gray |
| 1 | 3068b.dat | Tile 2 x 2 with Groove | Light Bluish Gray |
| 1 | 3069b.dat | Tile 1 x 2 with Groove | Dark Bluish Gray |

# Parts List

| Qty | Part | Description | Color |
|---|---|---|---|
| 1 | 3069b.dat | Tile 1 x 2 with Groove | Red |
| 3 | 3069b.dat | Tile 1 x 2 with Groove | Black |
| 3 | 3069b.dat | Tile 1 x 2 with Groove | Light Bluish Gray |
| 1 | 3069bpc3.dat | Tile 1 x 2 with Red "82" and Yellow and White Gauges Pattern | Light Bluish Gray |
| 2 | 3070b.dat | Tile 1 x 1 with Groove | Black |
| 1 | 3298.dat | Slope Brick 33 3 x 2 | Light Bluish Gray |
| 1 | 3460.dat | Plate 1 x 8 | Black |
| 2 | 3460.dat | Plate 1 x 8 | Dark Bluish Gray |
| 3 | 3460.dat | Plate 1 x 8 | Light Bluish Gray |
| 1 | 3622.dat | Brick 1 x 3 | Light Bluish Gray |
| 2 | 3623.dat | Plate 1 x 3 | Light Bluish Gray |
| 4 | 3660.dat | Slope Brick 45 2 x 2 Inverted | Light Bluish Gray |
| 2 | 3665.dat | Slope Brick 45 2 x 1 Inverted | Light Bluish Gray |
| 3 | 3666.dat | Plate 1 x 6 | Light Bluish Gray |
| 1 | 3680c01.dat | Turntable 2 x 2 Plate (Complete) | Black |
| 2 | 3705.dat | Technic Axle 4 | Black |
| 1 | 3710.dat | Plate 1 x 4 | Light Bluish Gray |
| 2 | 3747a.dat | Slope Brick 33 3 x 2 Inverted without Ribs between Studs | Light Bluish Gray |
| 4 | 3794b.dat | Plate 1 x 2 with Groove with 1 Centre Stud | Black |
| 6 | 3795.dat | Plate 2 x 6 | Dark Bluish Gray |
| 2 | 3823.dat | Windscreen 2 x 4 x 2 | Trans Black |
| 2 | 3832.dat | Plate 2 x 10 | Dark Bluish Gray |
| 1 | 3937.dat | Hinge 1 x 2 Base | Dark Bluish Gray |
| 1 | 3937.dat | Hinge 1 x 2 Base | Light Bluish Gray |
| 1 | 3938.dat | Hinge 1 x 2 Top | Light Bluish Gray |
| 2 | 3956.dat | Bracket 2 x 2 - 2 x 2 Up | Light Bluish Gray |
| 5 | 4070.dat | Brick 1 x 1 with Headlight | Light Bluish Gray |
| 2 | 4079.dat | Minifig Seat 2 x 2 | Black |
| 2 | 4081b.dat | Plate 1 x 1 with Clip Light Type 2 | Light Bluish Gray |
| 2 | 4085c.dat | Plate 1 x 1 with Clip Vertical Type 3 | Light Bluish Gray |
| 1 | 4150ps2.dat | Tile 2 x 2 Round with SW Sith Infiltrator Pattern | Light Bluish Gray |
| 3 | 4162.dat | Tile 1 x 8 | Light Bluish Gray |
| 2 | 4162.dat | Tile 1 x 8 | Black |
| 4 | 4175.dat | Plate 1 x 2 with Ladder | Light Bluish Gray |
| 1 | 4276b.dat | Hinge Plate 1 x 2 with 2 Fingers and Hollow Studs | Light Bluish Gray |
| 1 | 4286.dat | Slope Brick 33 3 x 1 | Light Bluish Gray |
| 2 | 4592c01.dat | Hinge Control Stick and Base (Complete) | Light Bluish Gray |
| 2 | 4864b.dat | Panel 1 x 2 x 2 with Hollow Studs | Trans Black |
| 1 | 6019.dat | Plate 1 x 1 with Clip Horizontal | Light Bluish Gray |
| 1 | 6134.dat | Hinge 2 x 2 Top | Light Bluish Gray |
| 4 | 6141.dat | Plate 1 x 1 Round | Trans Red |
| 2 | 6141.dat | Plate 1 x 1 Round | Black |
| 4 | 6141.dat | Plate 1 x 1 Round | Trans Neon Green |
| 4 | 6141.dat | Plate 1 x 1 Round | Light Bluish Gray |
| 8 | 6143.dat | Brick 2 x 2 Round Type 2 | Light Bluish Gray |
| 2 | 6231.dat | Panel 1 x 1 x 1 Corner with Rounded Corners | Light Bluish Gray |
| 4 | 6249.dat | Brick 2 x 4 with Pins | Light Bluish Gray |
| 1 | 6636.dat | Tile 1 x 6 | Dark Bluish Gray |
| 1 | 6636.dat | Tile 1 x 6 | Light Bluish Gray |
| 2 | 6636.dat | Tile 1 x 6 | Black |
| 2 | 30010.dat | Panel 1 x 2 x 1 with Square Corners | Light Bluish Gray |
| 6 | 30071.dat | Brick 1 x 1 | Light Bluish Gray |
| 6 | 30136.dat | Brick 1 x 2 Log | Light Bluish Gray |
| 2 | 30283.dat | Slope Brick 45 6 x 4 Double Inverted with Open Center | Light Bluish Gray |
| 9 | 30285.dat | Wheel Hub 14.8 x 16.8 with Centre Groove | White |
| 2 | 30383.dat | Hinge Plate 1 x 2 Locking with Single Finger On Top | Dark Bluish Gray |
| 9 | 30391.dat | Tyre 30.4 x 14 | Black |
| 1 | 30395.dat | Hook with Towball | Light Bluish Gray |
| 1 | 30396.dat | Hinge 1 x 2 Locking with Towball Socket | Black |
| 4 | 30413.dat | Panel 1 x 4 x 1 | Light Bluish Gray |
| 2 | 30554.dat | Hinge Arm Locking with Single and Dual Fingers | Light Bluish Gray |
| 1 | 44237.dat | Brick 2 x 6 | Dark Bluish Gray |

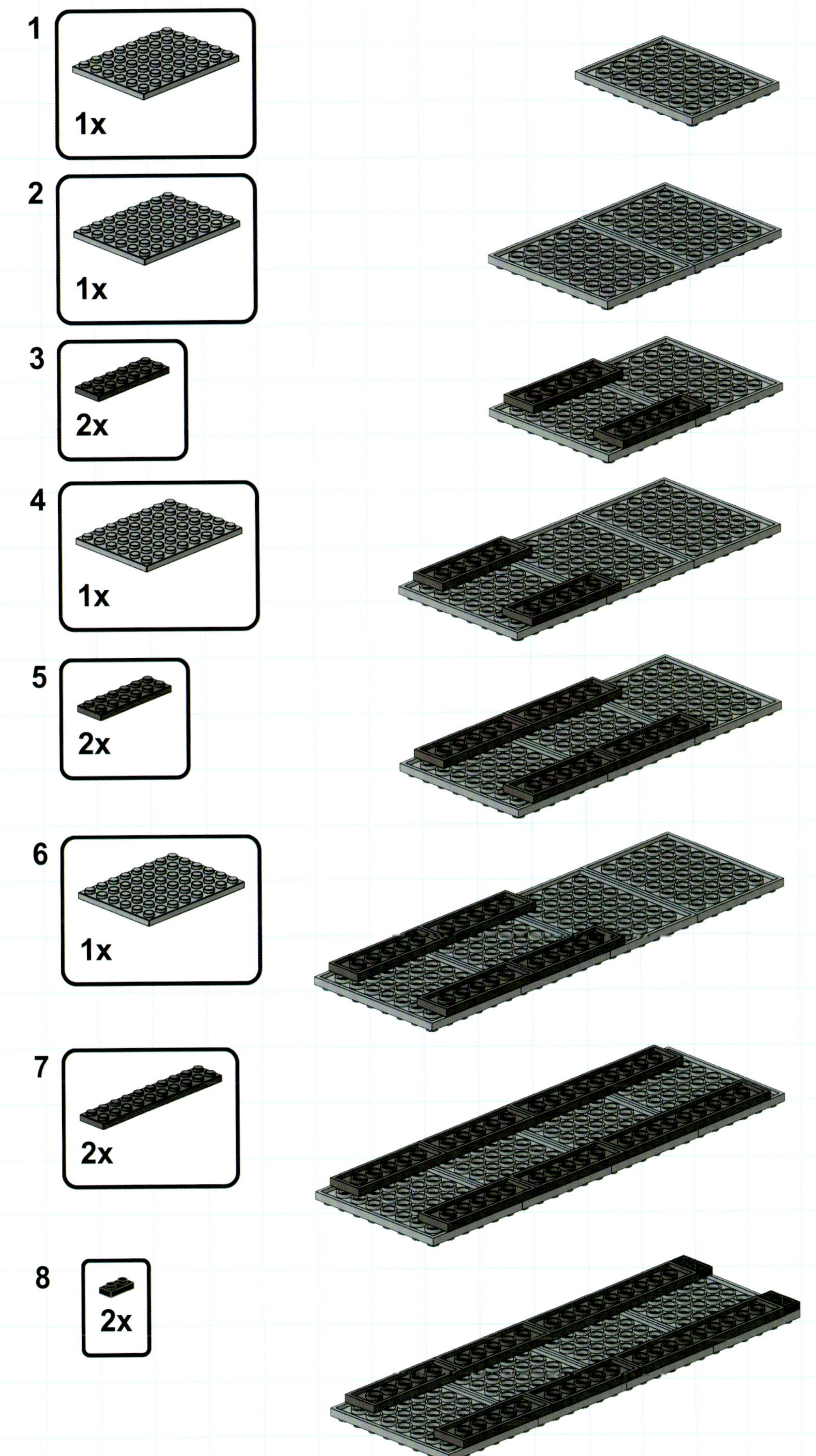
1
1x
2
1x
3
2x
4
1x
5
2x
6
1x
7
2x
8
2x

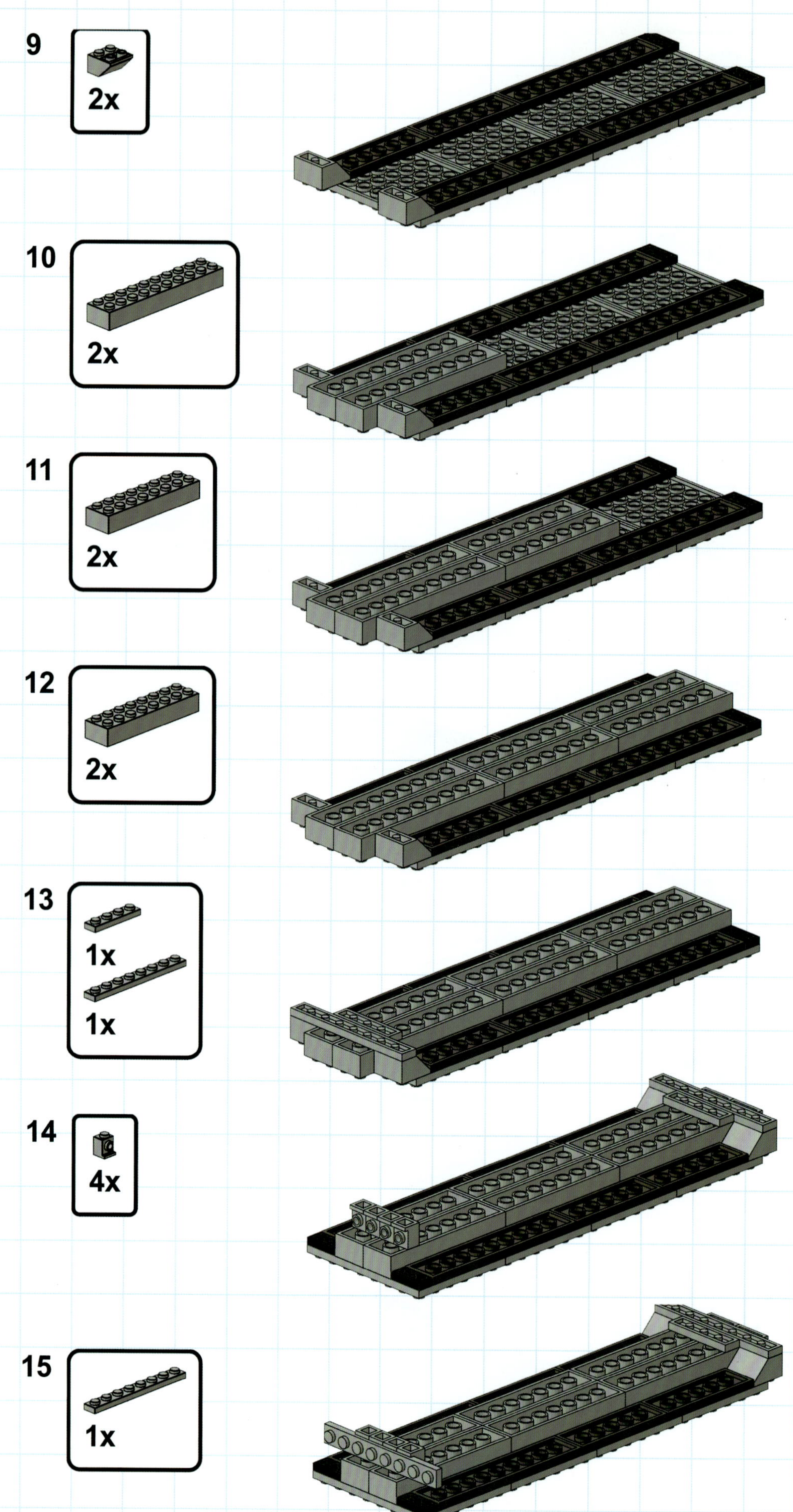
9
2x
10
2x
11
2x
12
2x
13
1x
1x
14
4x
15
1x

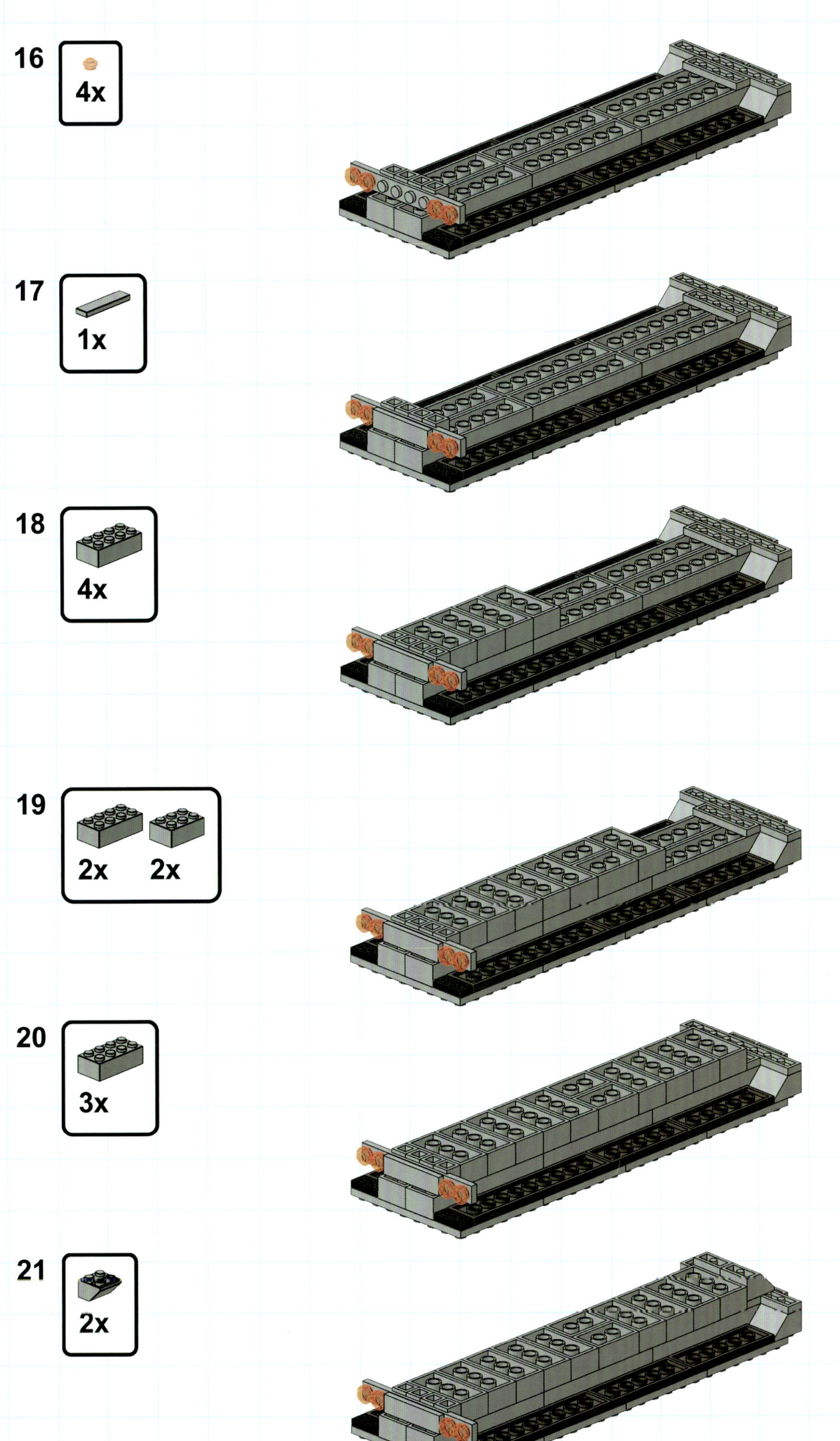

16
4x
17
1x
18
4x
19
2x
2x
20
3x
21
2x

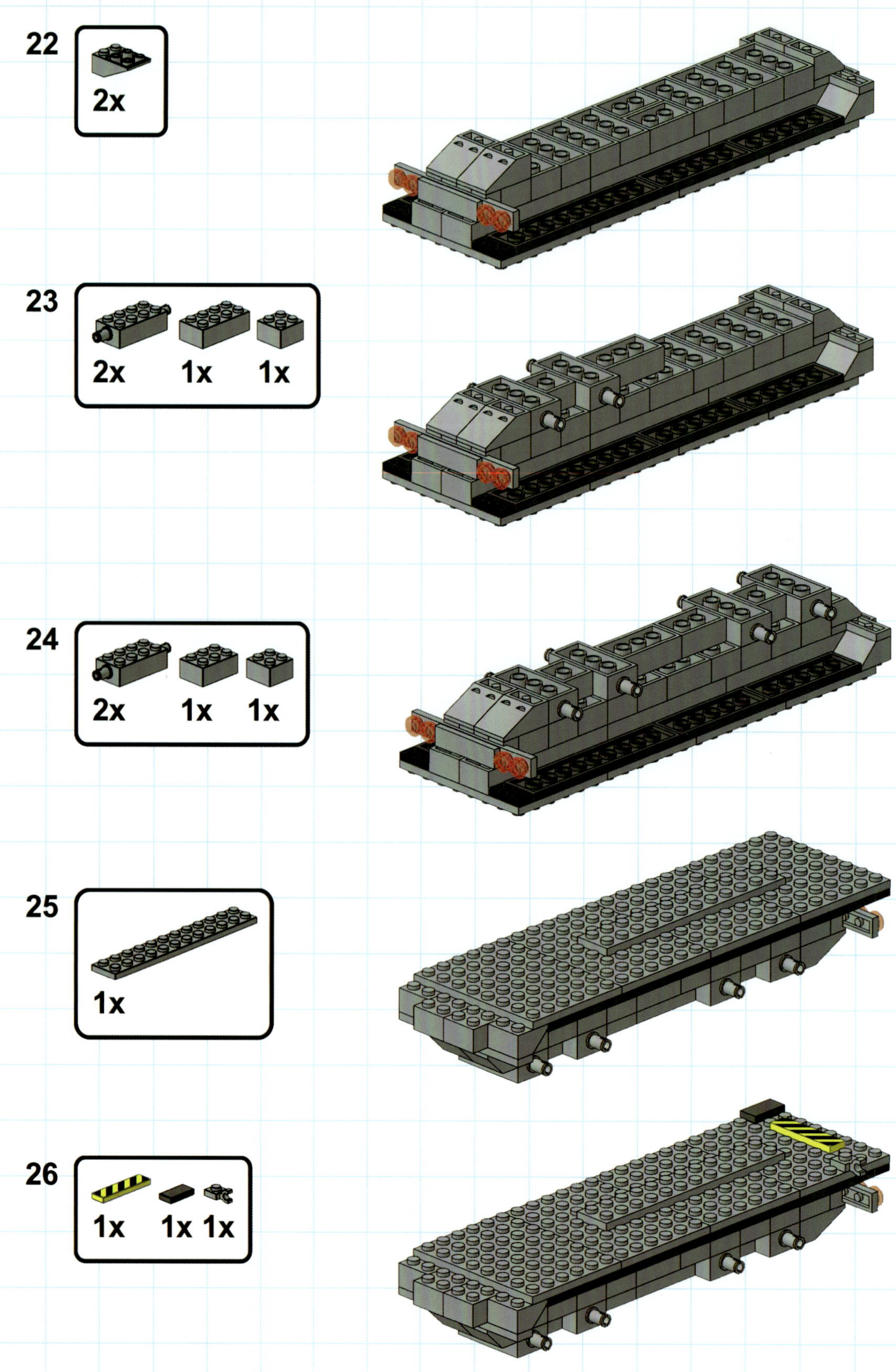
22
2x
23
2x
1x
1x
24
2x
1x
1x
25
1x
26
1x
1x 1x

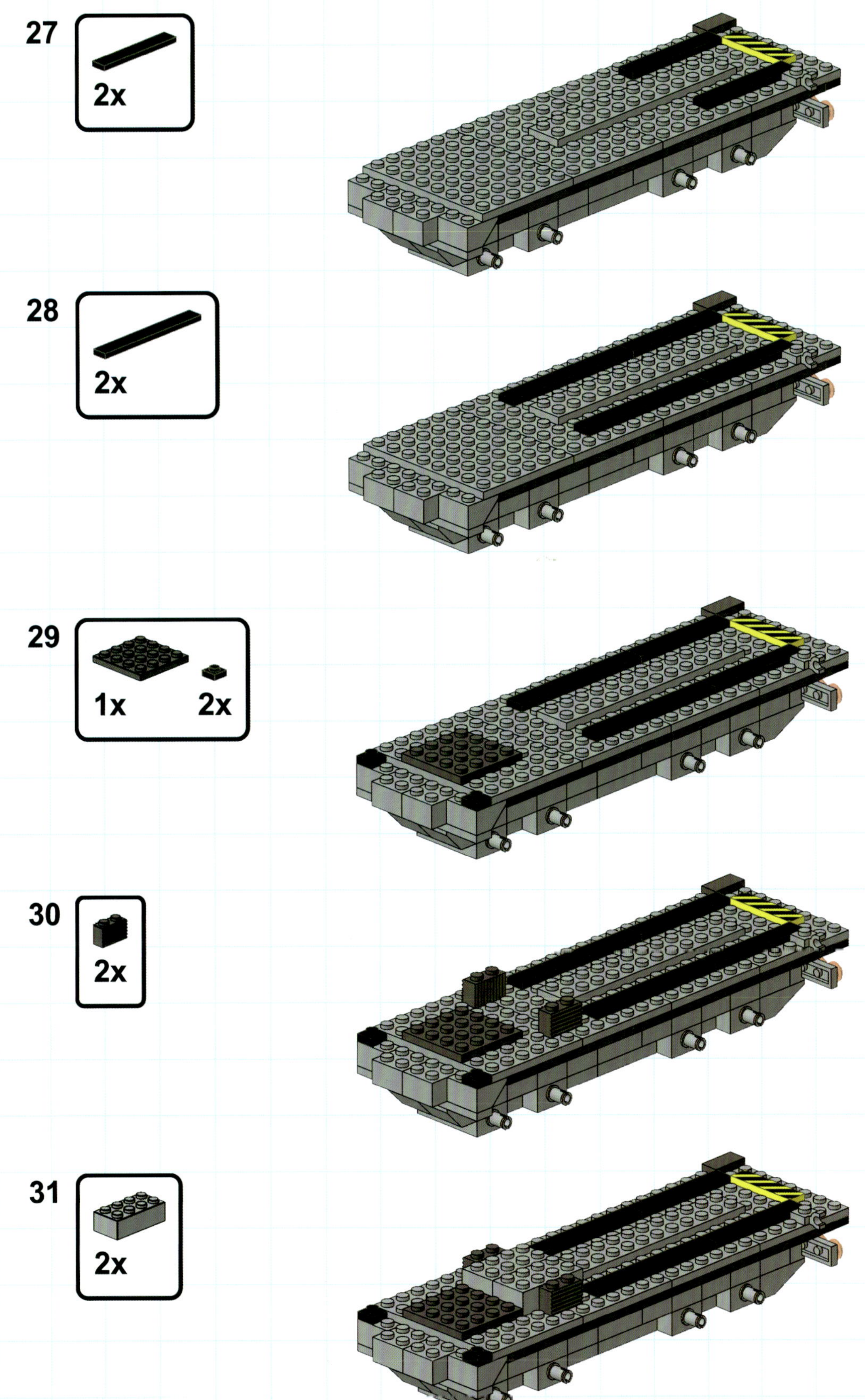
27
2x
28
2x
29
1x
2x
30
2x
31
2x

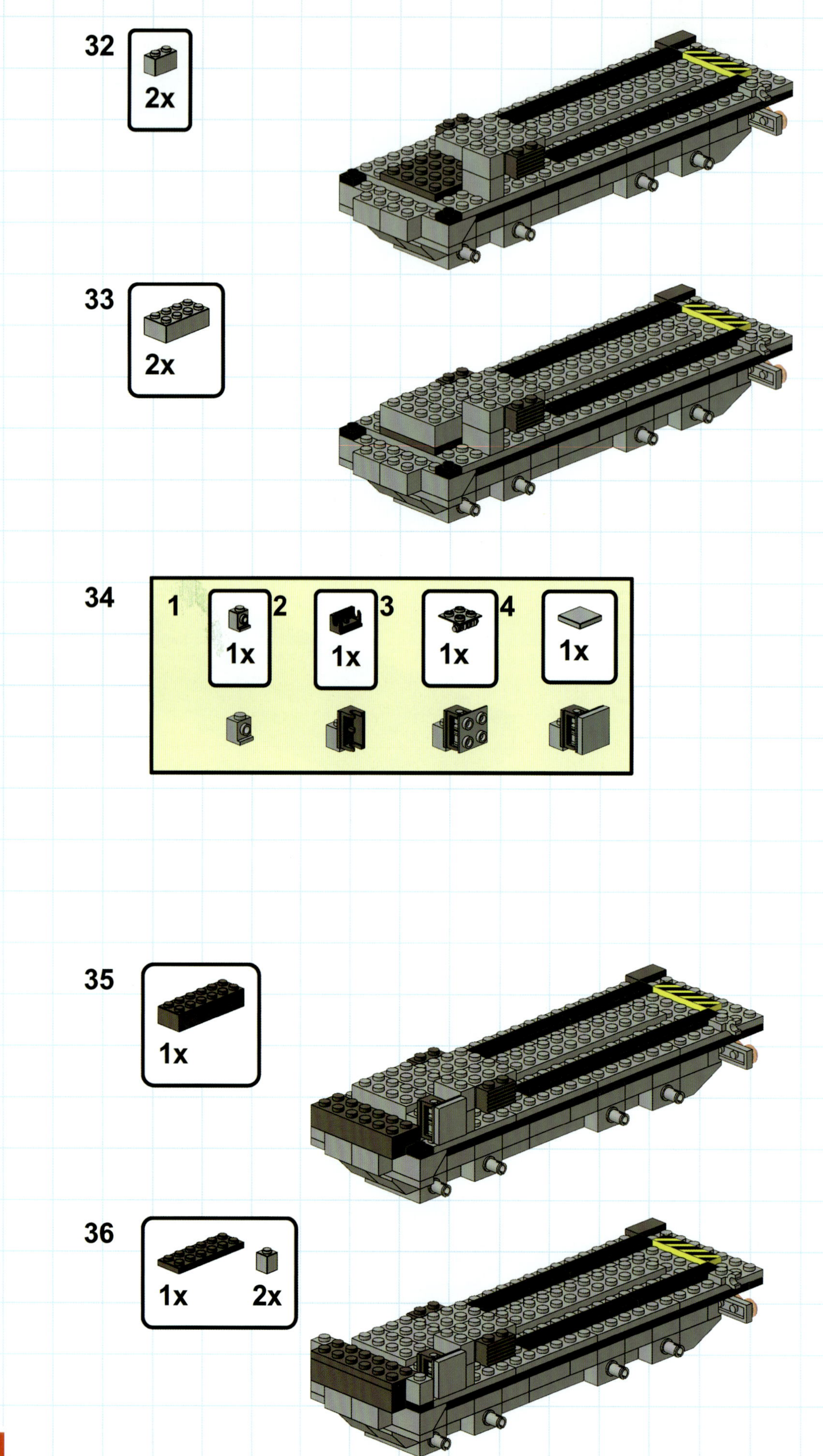
32
2x
33
2x
34
1
1x
2
1x
3
1x
4
1x
35
1x
36
1x
2x

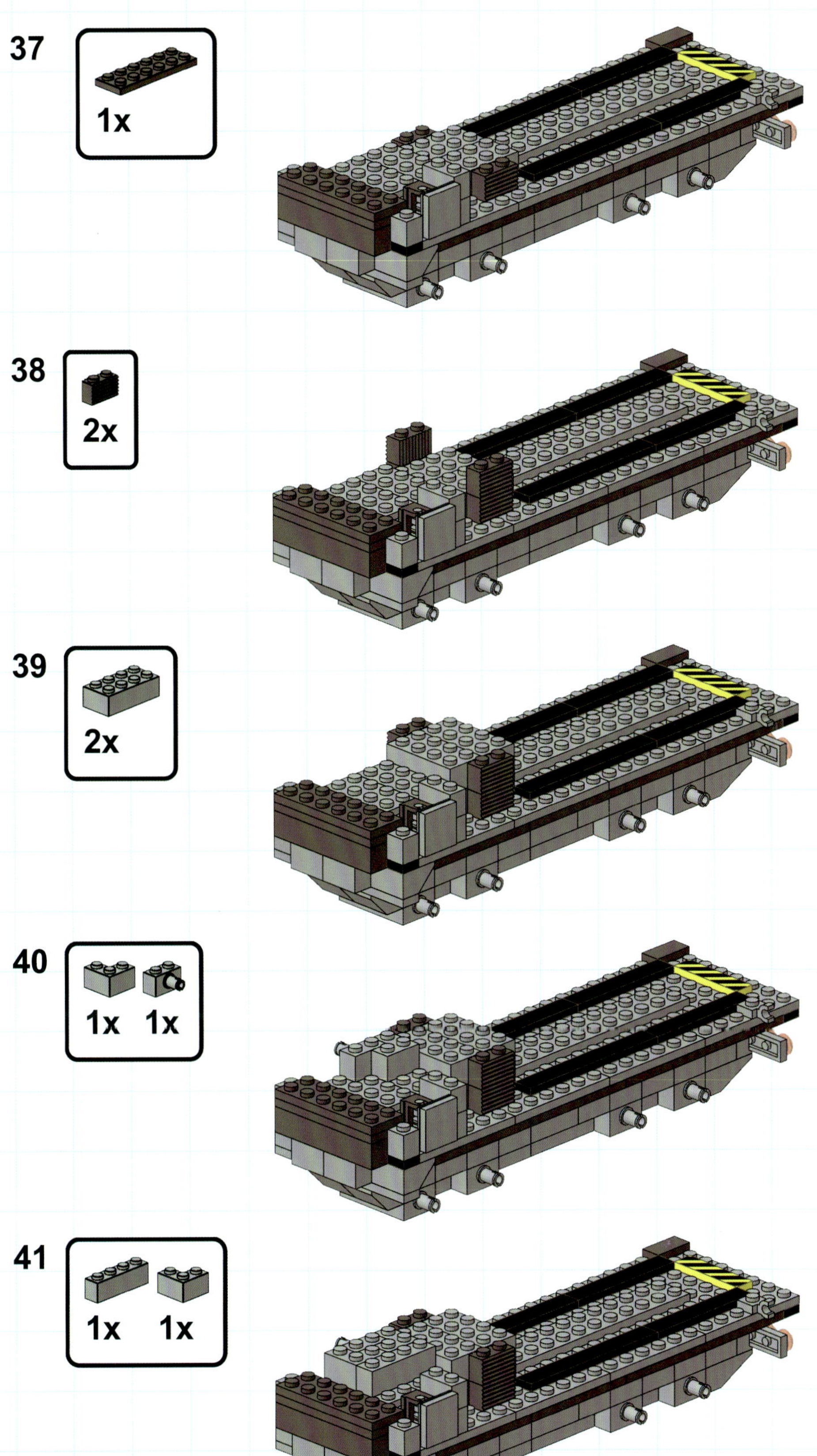
37
1x
38
2x
39
2x
40
1x
1x
41
1x
1x

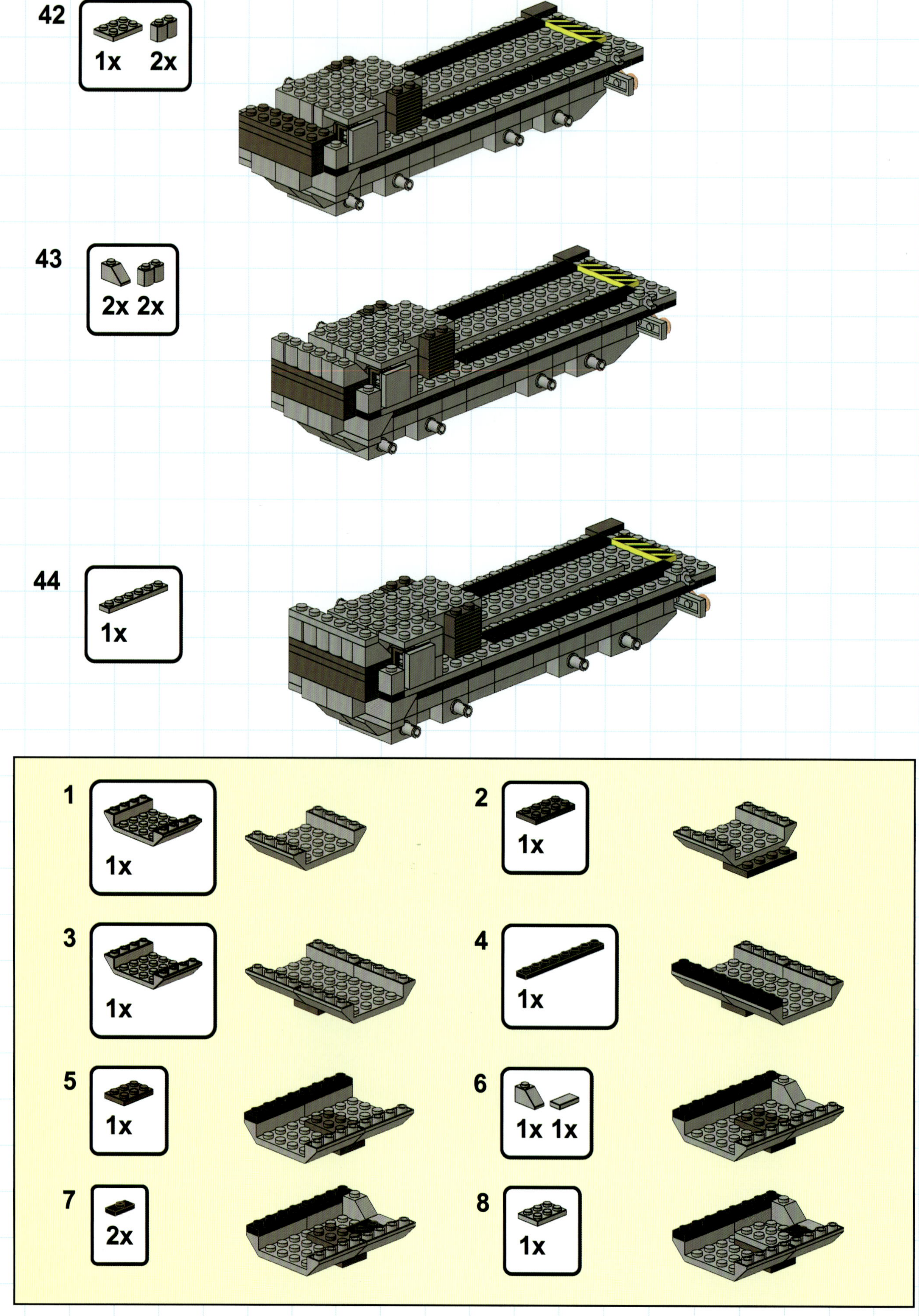
42
1x 2x
43
2x 2x
44
1x
1
1x
2
1x
3
1x
4
1x
5
1x
6
1x 1x
7
2x
8
1x

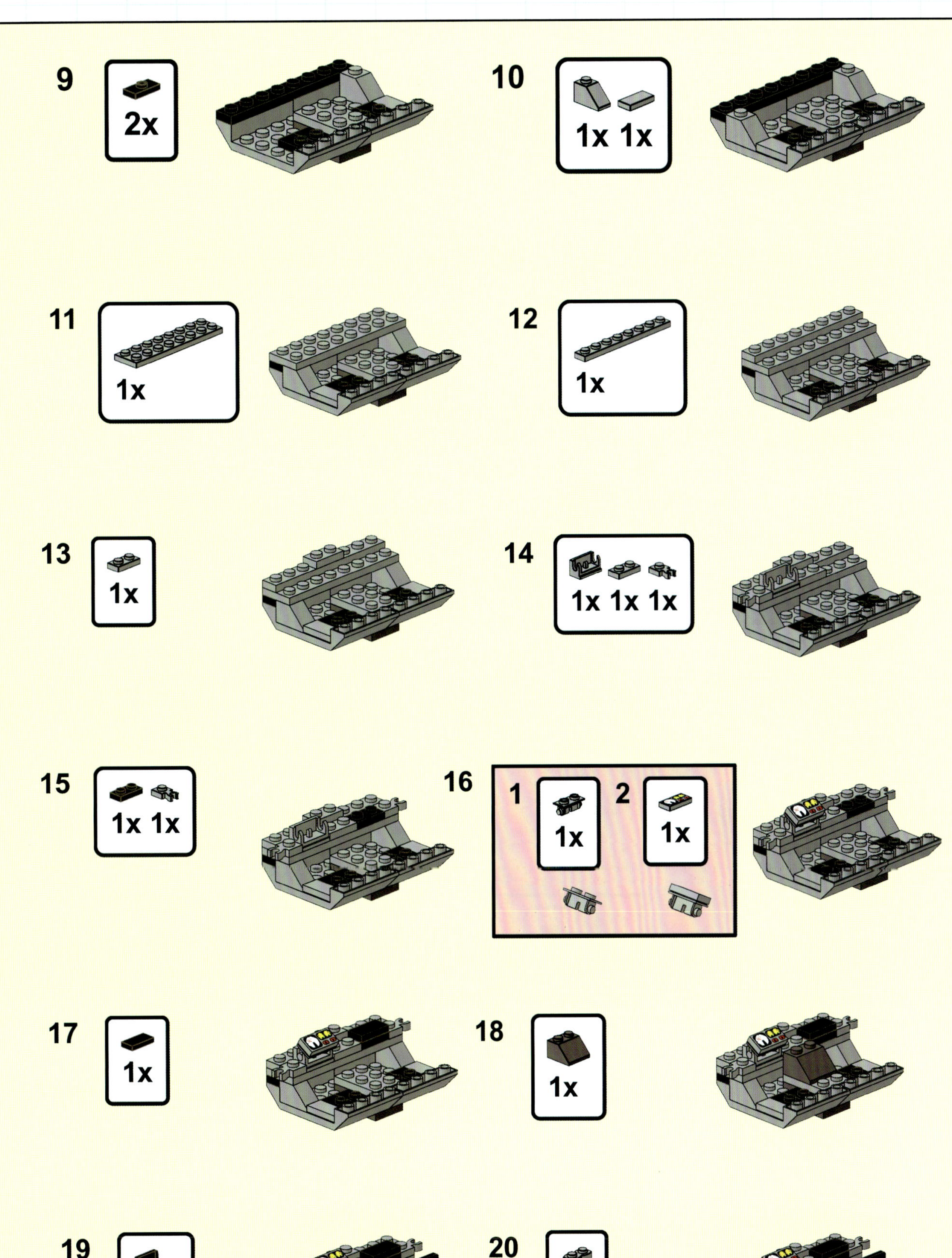
9
2x
10
1x 1x
11
1x
12
1x
13
1x
14
1x 1x 1x
15
1x 1x
16
1
1x
2
1x
17
1x
18
1x
19
2x
20
1x

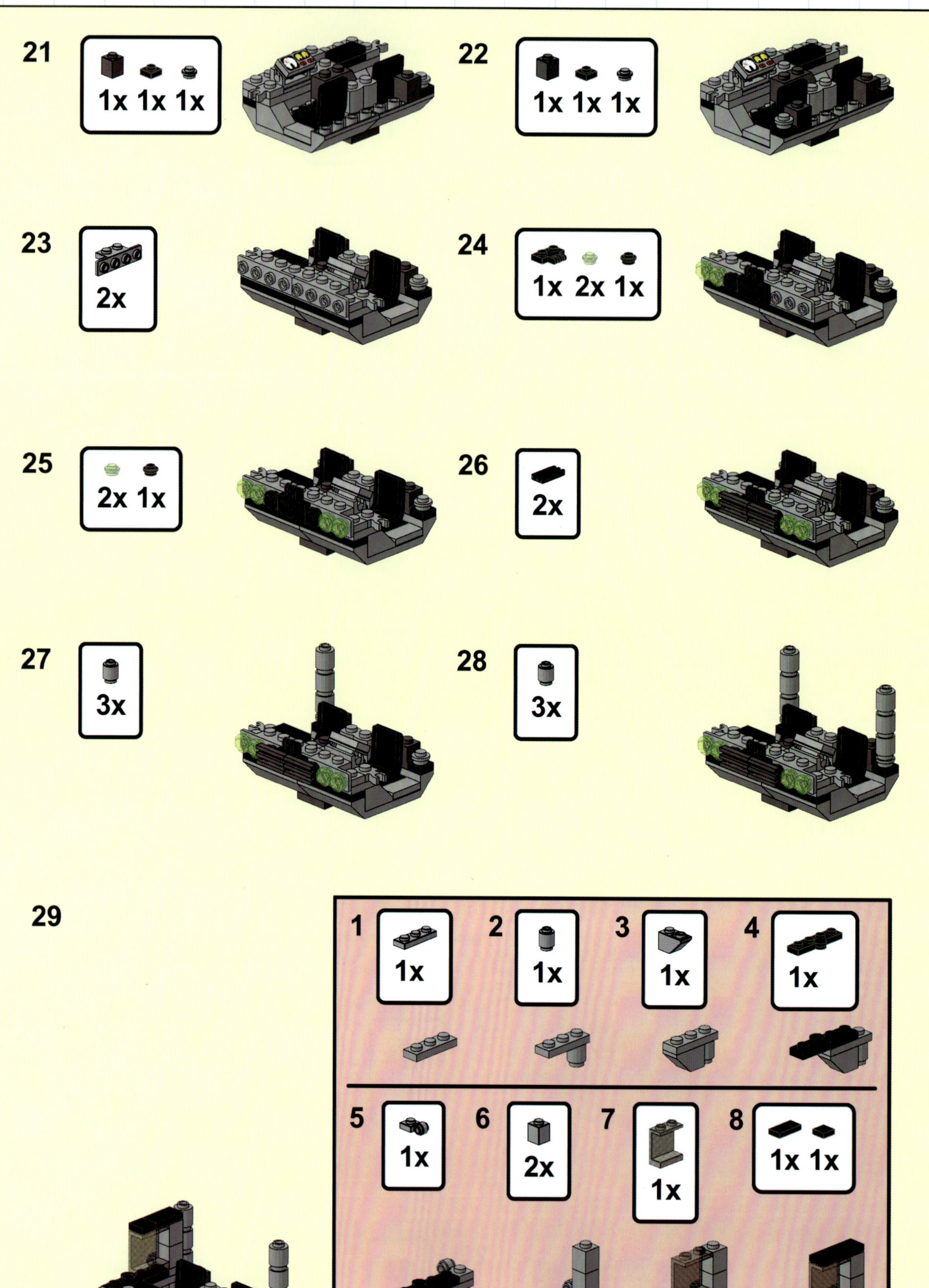
21
1x 1x 1x
22
1x 1x 1x
23
2x
24
1x 2x 1x
25
2x 1x
26
2x
27
3x
28
3x
29
1
1x
2
1x
3
1x
4
1x
5
1x
6
2x
7
1x
8
1x 1x

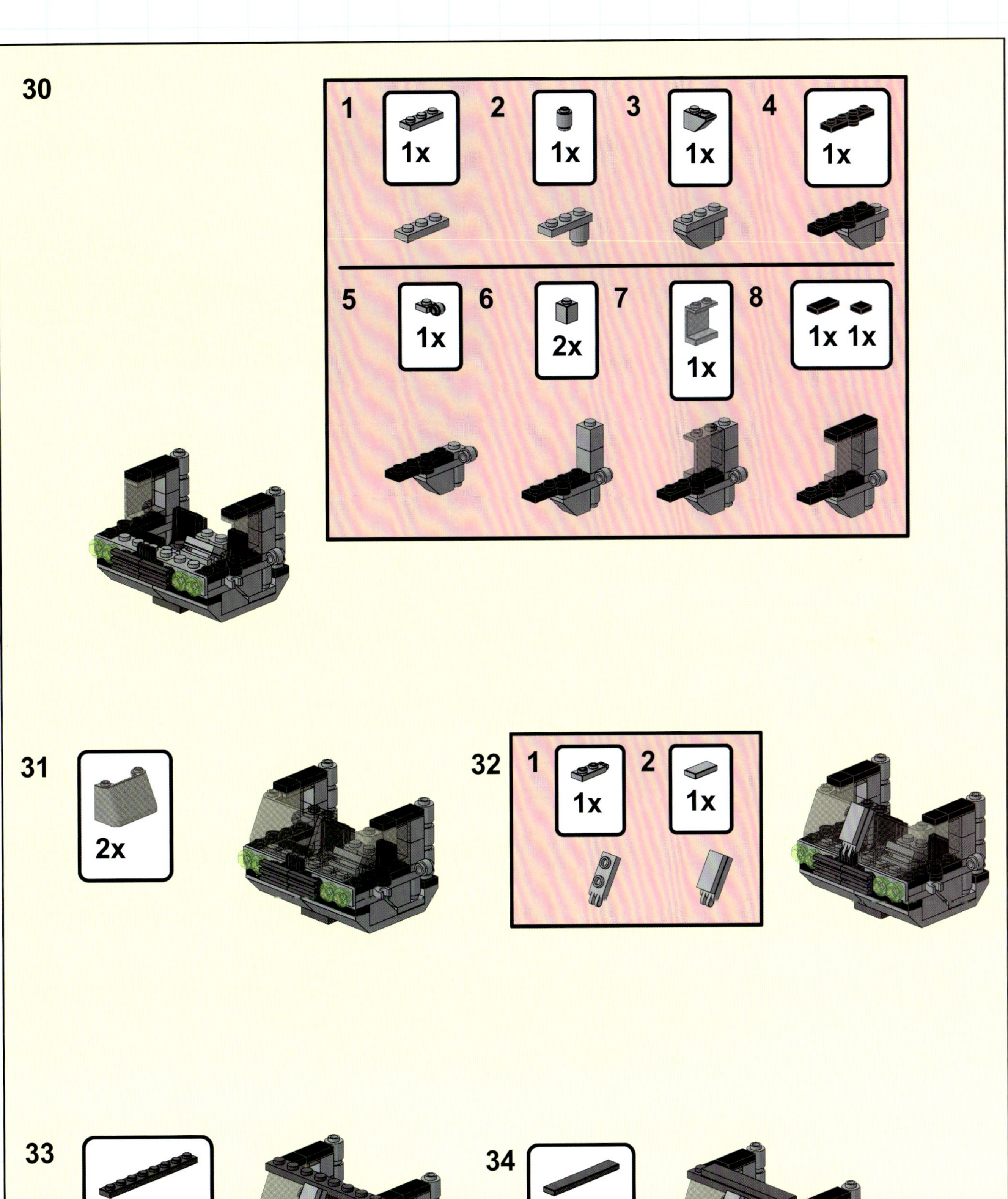


33

1x

34

1x

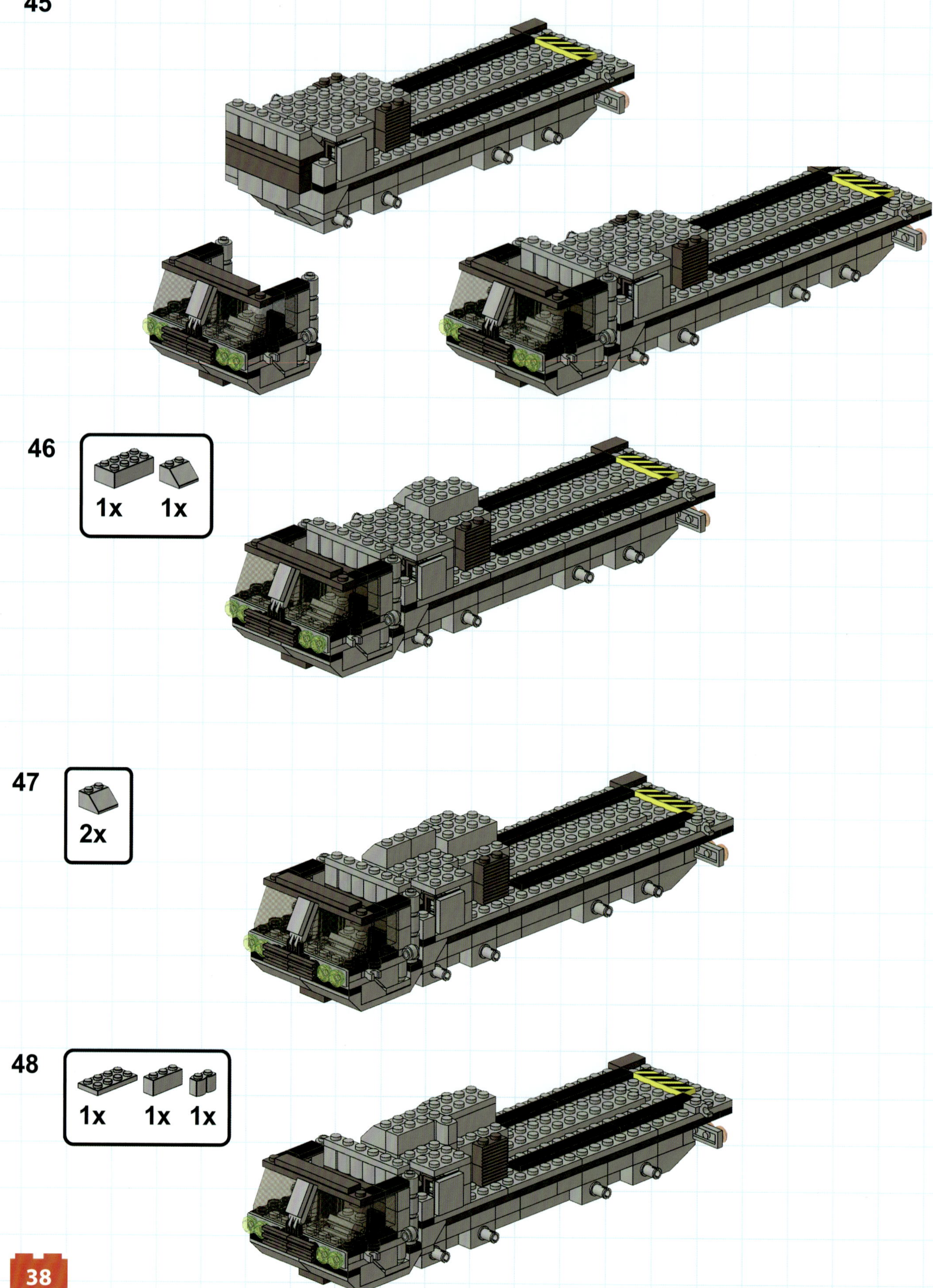
45
46
1x
1x
47
2x
48
1x
1x
1x

49

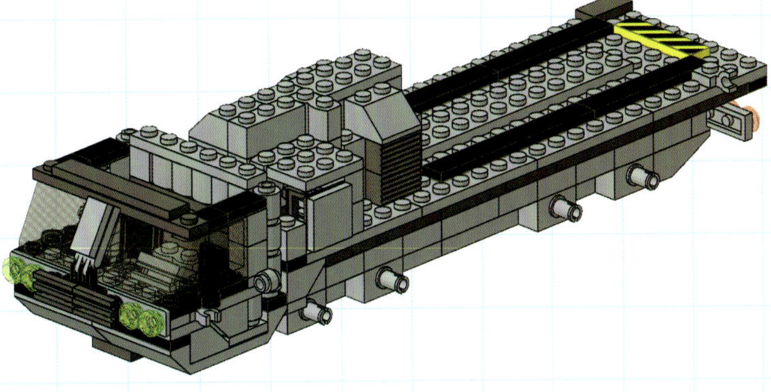

50

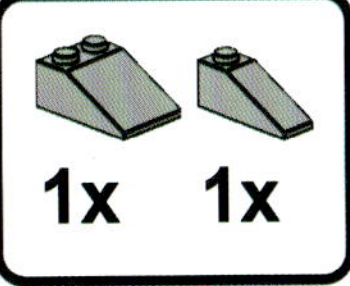


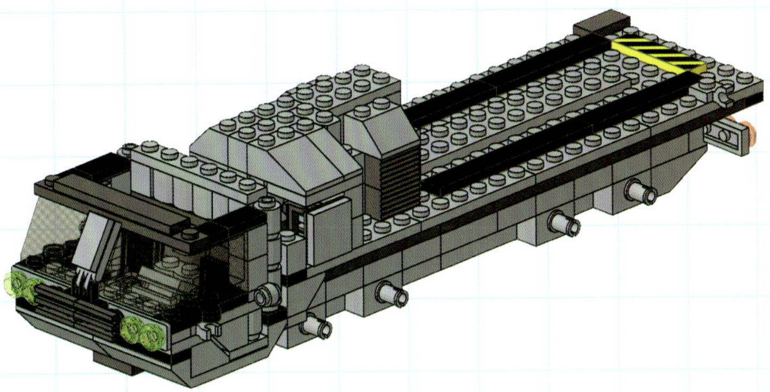

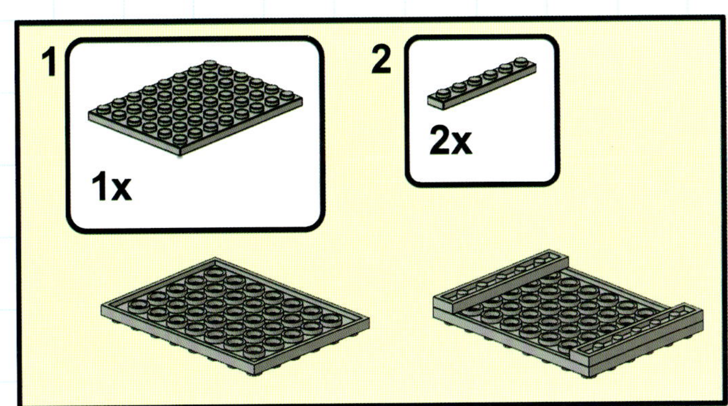


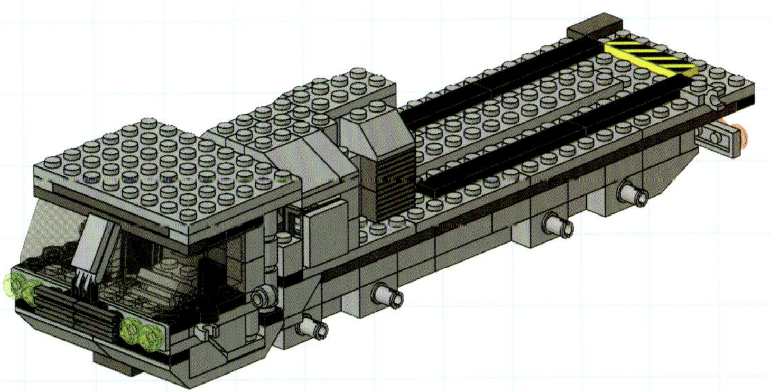

1
1x
2
1x
3
1x
4
1x
5
1x

1x
2x

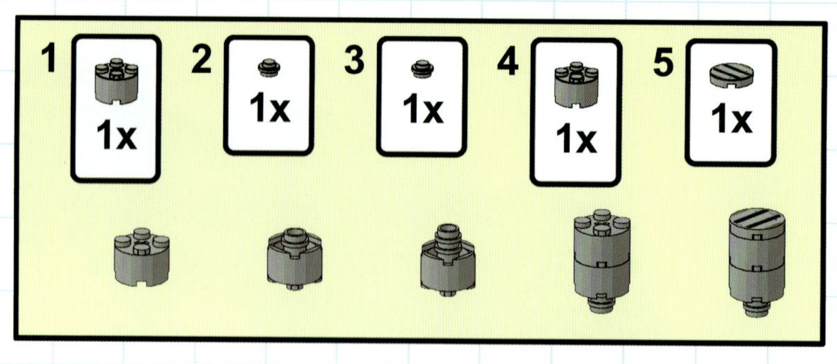

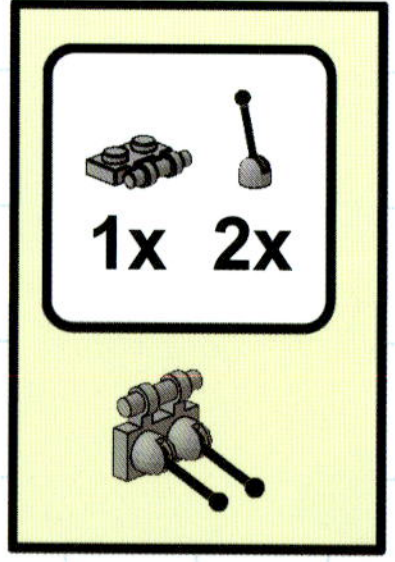

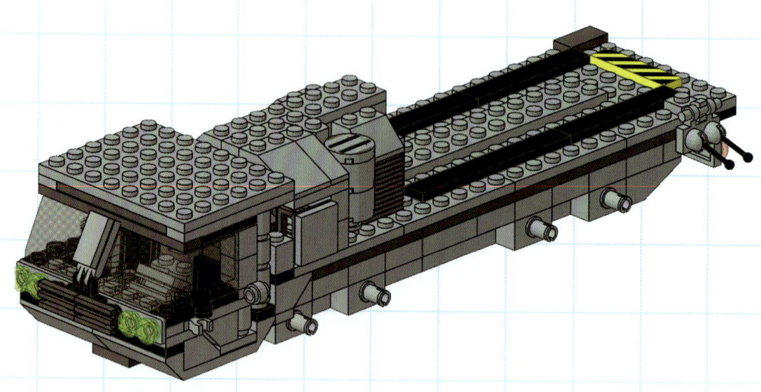

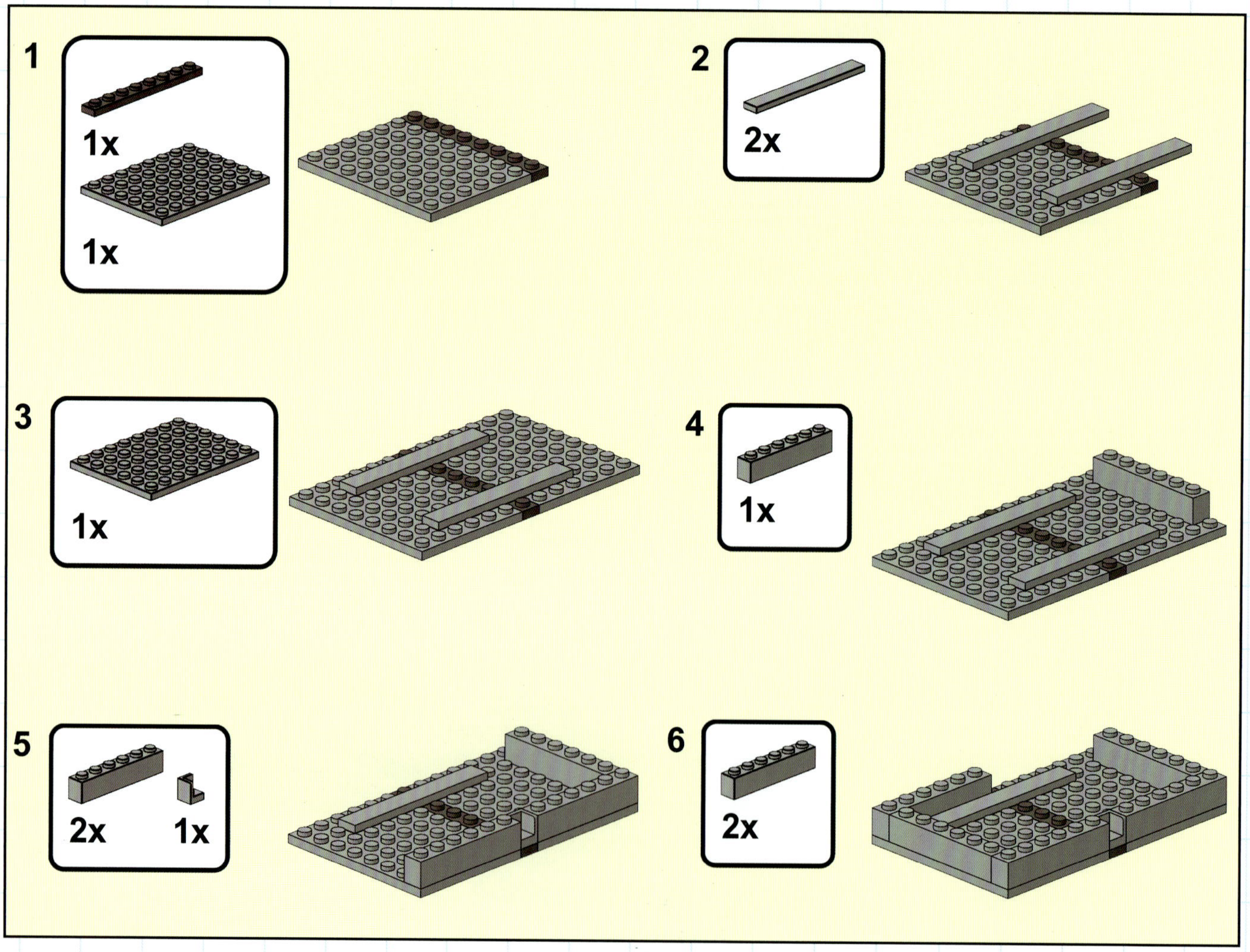

1
1x
1x
2
2x
3
1x
4
1x
5
2x
1x
6
2x

7

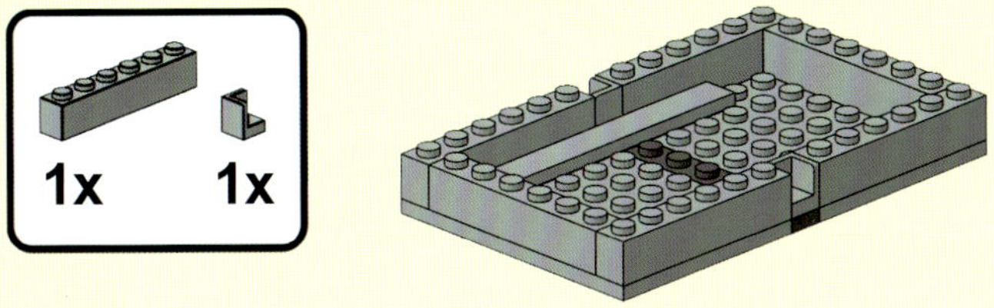

1x 1x

8

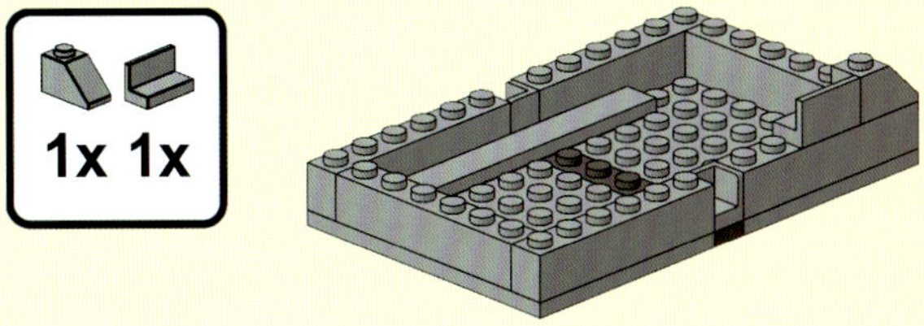

1x 1x

9

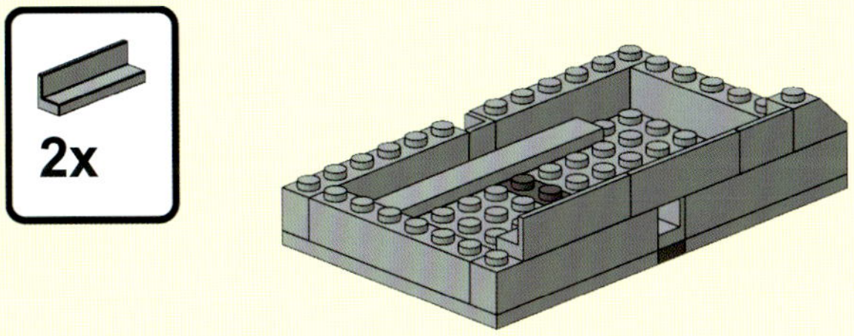

2x

10

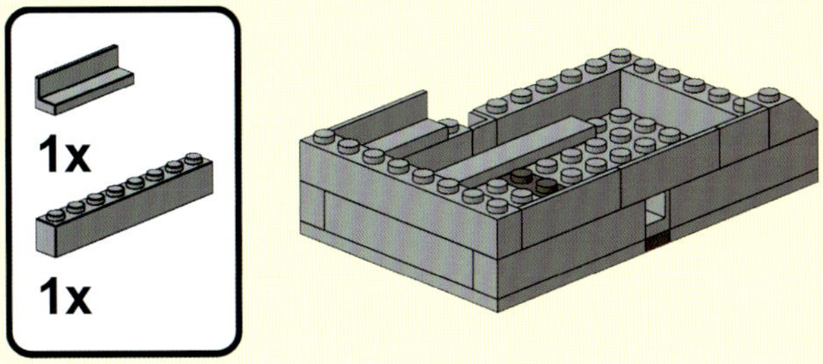

1x

1x

11

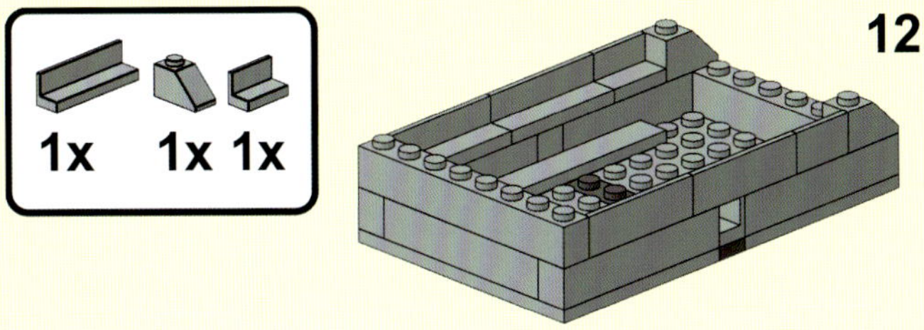

1x 1x 1x

12

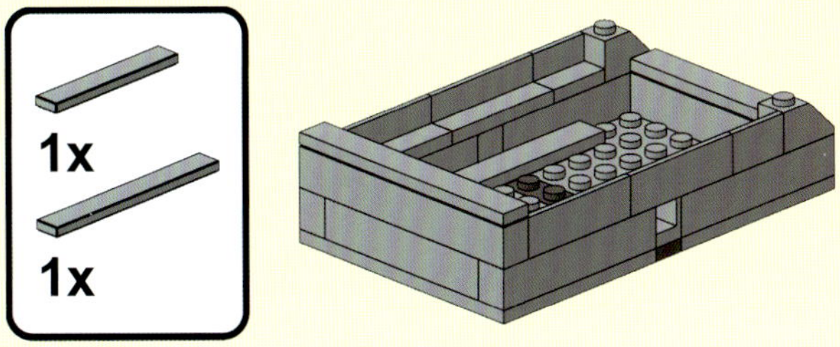

1x

1x

53

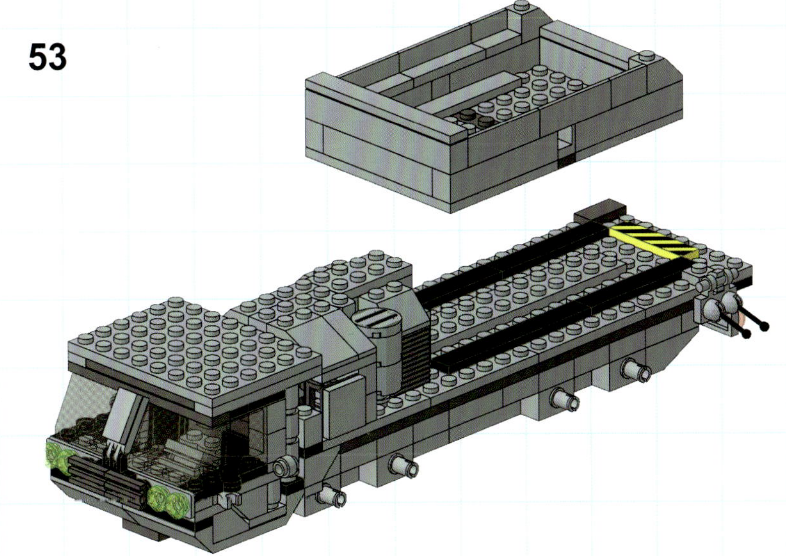

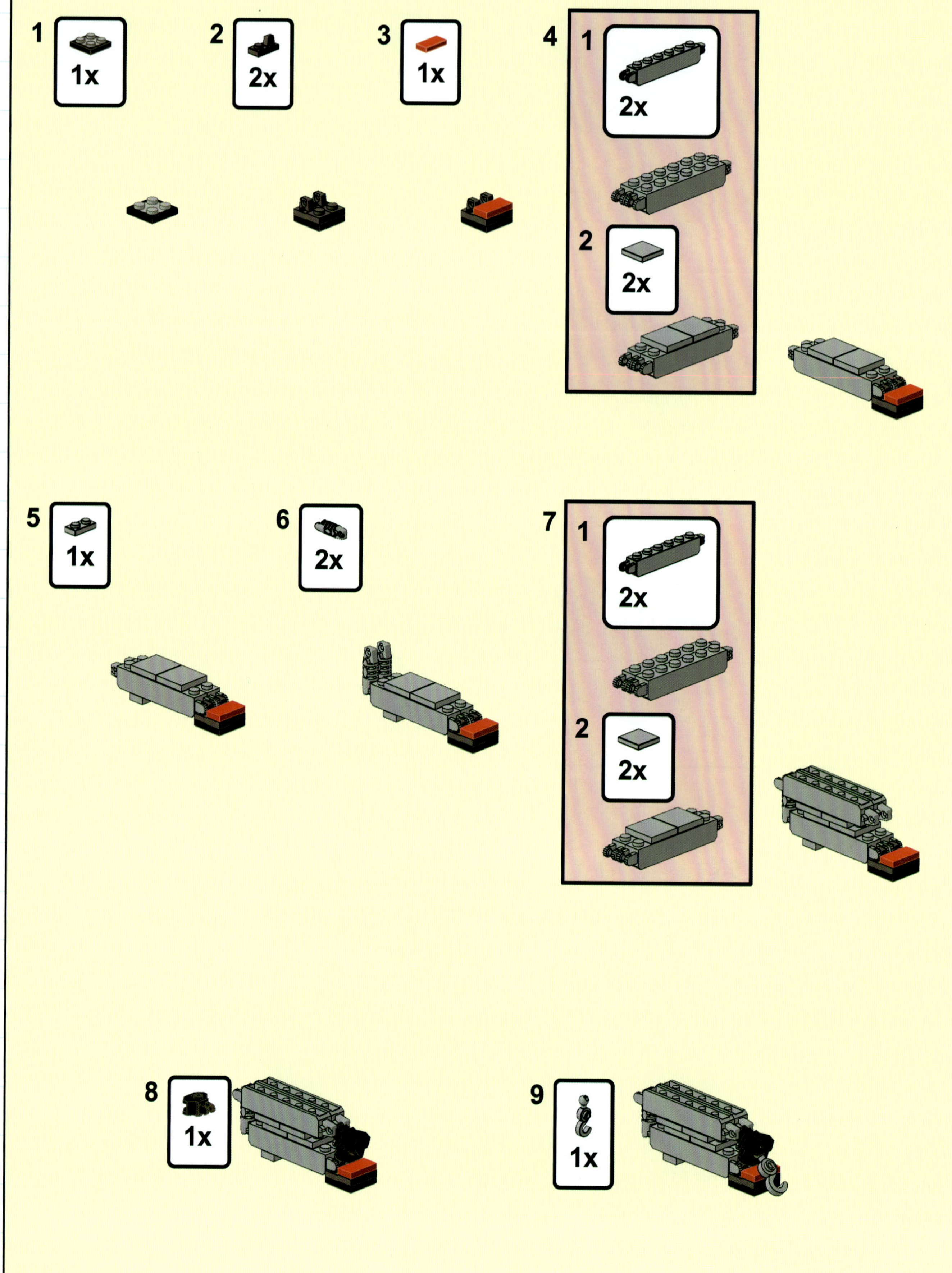
1
1x
2
2x
3
1x
4
1
2x
2
2x
5
1x
6
2x
7
1
2x
2
2x
8
1x
9
1x

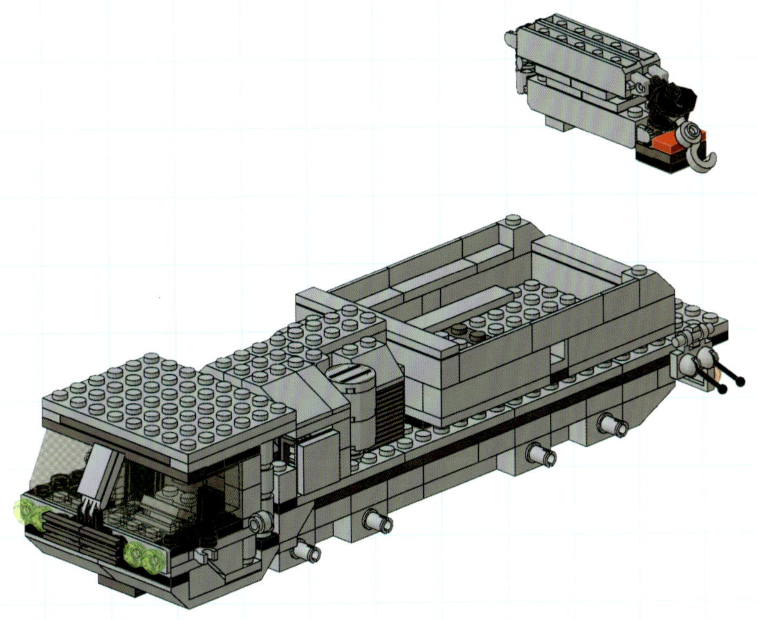

54

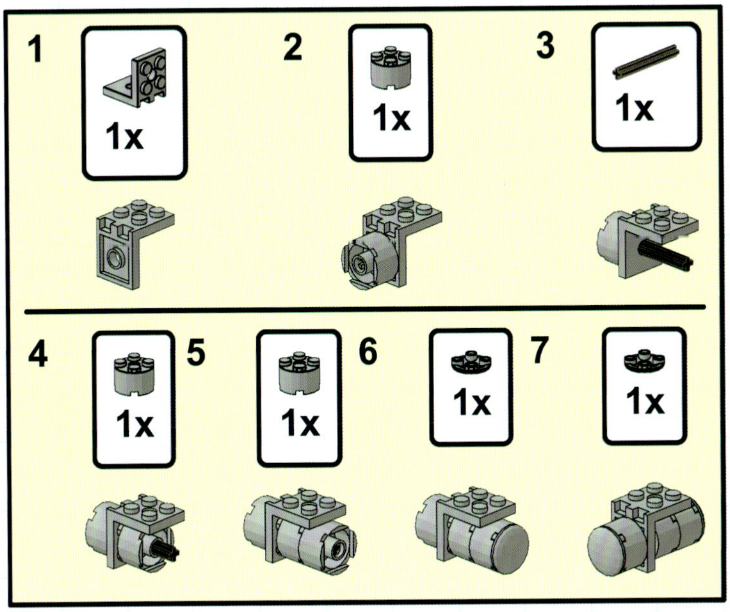

1 1x

2 1x

3 1x

4 1x

5 1x

6 1x

7 1x

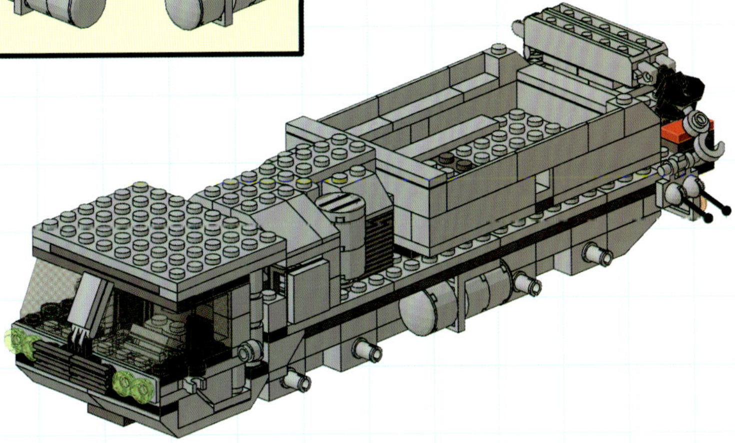

55

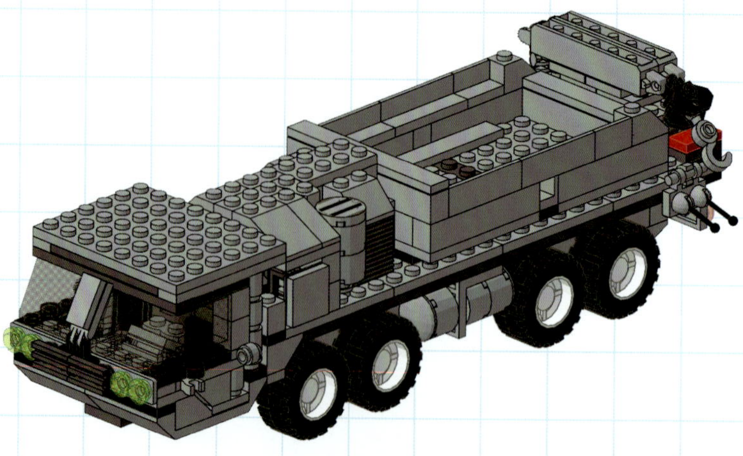

56

2x

57

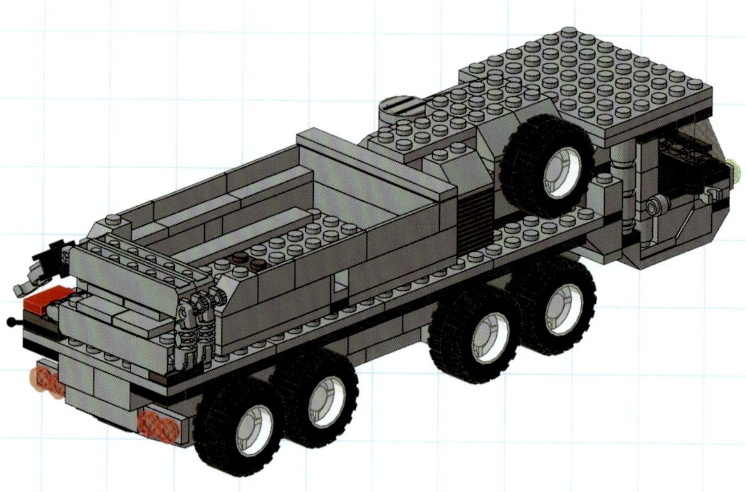

58

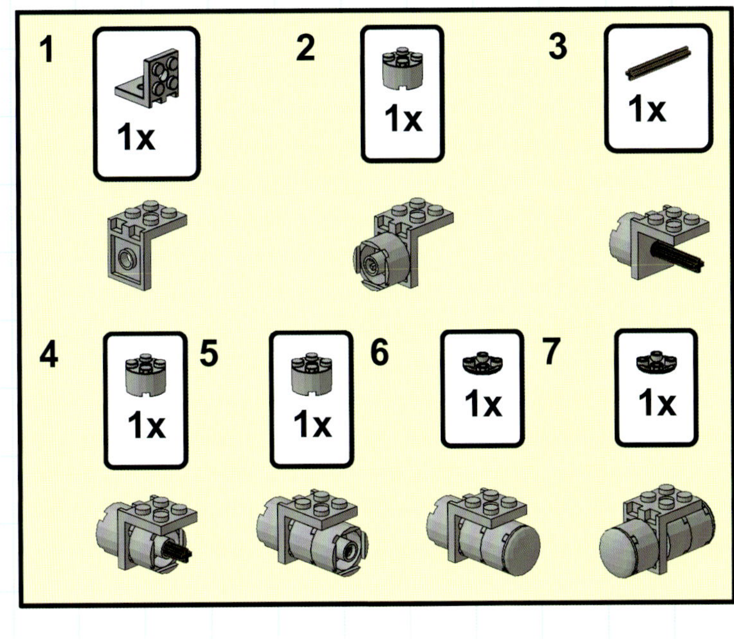

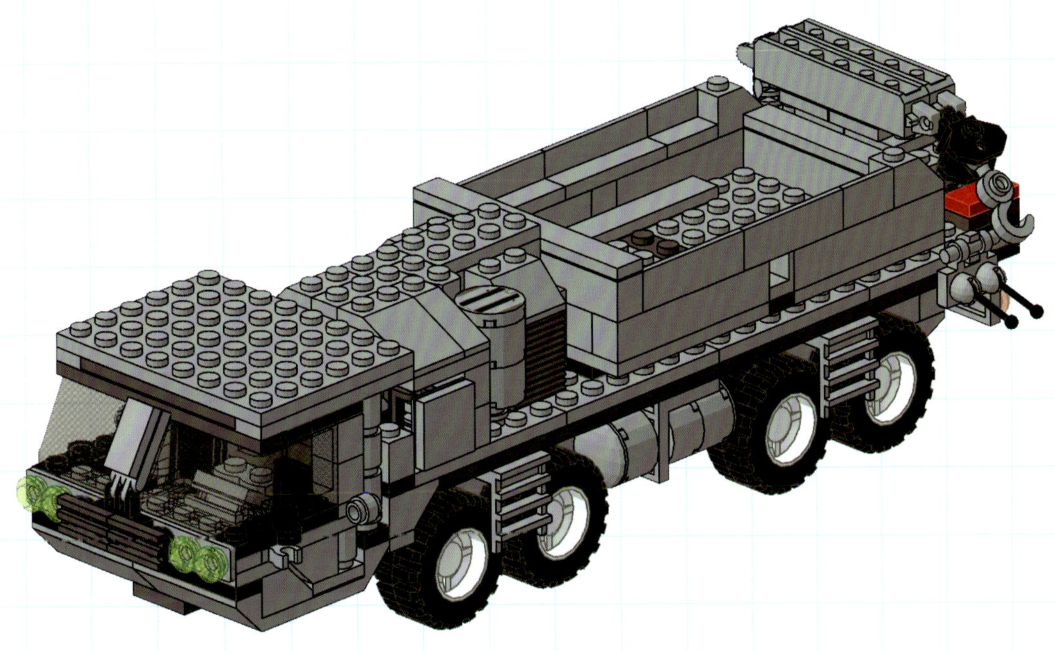

# Mini Deep Sea Diorama

*Design and Instructions by Christopher Deck*

*This article and model first appeared in Issue 10 of* BrickJournal.

With more than one hundred pieces, this mini diorama has slightly more parts than an average mini model. It consists of the sea bottom with a small shipwreck, a giant spider crab, a sixgill shark (those could be found within depths of more than 2,000 meters) and a small yellow submarine exploring the sea ground.

Building this was quite fun, as it's different from what I usually build. I especially enjoyed building the small creatures, although I have to admit that it cost me some time and many attempts to come up with a micro shark design which looked satisfying enough. Those new 1x1 slopes were really helpful for that. The spider crab uses a modified octagonal plate and lots of droid arms attached around it. For the little yellow sub I wanted to use octagonal elements because they provide a typical submarine look and echo the spirit of the former underwater themes in which they were used.

Crab, shark and sub, together with the sea ground and its rocks, plants and shipwreck, create this nice little underwater scene. With this, I am done for this time. I wish you happy building!

# Parts List

## SEA BOTTOM

| Qty. | Part | Description | Color |
|---|---|---|---|
| 1 | 3867.dat | Baseplate 16 x 16 | Tan |
| 6 | 3062b.dat | Brick 1 x 1 Round with Hollow Stud | Reddish-Brown |
| 1 | 3010.dat | Brick 1 x 4 | Md-Stone-Gray |
| 1 | 2357.dat | Brick 2 x 2 Corner | Md-Stone-Gray |
| 2 | 3001.dat | Brick 2 x 4 | Md-Stone-Gray |
| 2 | 6188.dat | Cone 1 x 1 | Trans-Green |
| 3 | 6126.dat | Minifig Flame | Trans-Green |
| 18 | 4728.dat | Plant Flower 2 x 2 | Trans-Purple |
| 1 | 30093.dat | Plant Sea Grass | Trans-Green |
| 4 | 3024.dat | Plate 1 x 1 | Trans-Green |
| 3 | 3794.dat | Plate 1 x 2 with 1 Stud | Reddish-Brown |
| 1 | 3623.dat | Plate 1 x 3 | Reddish-Brown |
| 1 | 3710.dat | Plate 1 x 4 | Reddish-Brown |
| 1 | 3666.dat | Plate 1 x 6 | Reddish-Brown |
| 1 | 30385.dat | Rock 1 x 1 Crystal 5 Point | Trans-Neon-Green |
| 1 | 3747.dat | Slope Brick 33 3 x 2 Inverted | Reddish-Brown |
| 8 | 3665.dat | Slope Brick 45 2 x 1 Inverted | Reddish-Brown |
| 1 | 3039.dat | Slope Brick 45 2 x 2 | Reddish-Brown |
| 1 | 3039.dat | Slope Brick 45 2 x 2 | Md-Stone-Gray |
| 2 | 3660.dat | Slope Brick 45 2 x 2 Inverted | Reddish-Brown |

## SHARK

| Qty | Part | Description | Color |
|---|---|---|---|
| 1 | 4733.dat | Brick 1 x 1 with Studs on Four Sides | Dk-Stone-Gray |
| 2 | 47905.dat | Brick 1 x 1 with Studs on Two Opposite Sides | Dk-Stone-Gray |
| 1 | 6188.dat | Cone 1 x 1 | Dk-Stone-Gray |
| 5 | 54200.dat | Slope Brick 31 1 x 1 x 2/3 | Dk-Stone-Gray |
| 1 | 3040b.dat | Slope Brick 45 2 x 1 | Dk-Stone-Gray |

## CRAB

| Qty | Part | Description | Color |
|---|---|---|---|
| 1 | 54196.dat | Dish 2 x 2 | Black |
| 6 | 30377.dat | Minifig Mechanical Arm | Black |
| 2 | 59230.dat | Minifig Mechanical Arm Straight | Black |
| 2 | 4073.dat | Plate 1 x 1 Round | Trans-Orange |
| 1 | 33291.dat | Plate 1 x 1 Round with Tabs | Trans-Clear |
| 1 | 2540.dat | Plate 1 x 2 with Handle | Black |
| 1 | 30033.dat | Plate 2 x 2 with Rod Frame Octagonal | Black |
| 2 | 2555.dat | Tile 1 x 1 with Clip | Black |

## SUB

| Qty | Part | Description | Color |
|---|---|---|---|
| 2 | 48729.dat | Bar 1.5L with Clip | Black |
| 1 | 3941.dat | Brick 2 x 2 Round | Trans-Clear |
| 1 | 6042.dat | Brick 2 x 2 x 3 & 1/3 Octagonal With Side Studs | Yellow |
| 1 | 30663.dat | Car Steering Wheel Large | Black |
| 2 | 6188.dat | Cone 1 x 1 | Black |
| 1 | 6039.dat | Cone 2 x 2 x 1 & 2/3 Octagonal | Yellow |
| 1 | 30367.dat | Cylinder 2 x 2 with Dome Top | Yellow |
| 1 | 54196.dat | Dish 2 x 2 | Trans-Clear |
| 2 | 53989.dat | Minifig Mechanical Arm with Clip and Rod Hole | Black |
| 2 | 4073.dat | Plate 1 x 1 Round | Trans-Yellow |
| 1 | 4073.dat | Plate 1 x 1 Round | Trans-Clear |
| 2 | 2540.dat | Plate 1 x 2 with Handle | Yellow |
| 1 | 4599.dat | Tap 1 x 1 | Black |

1

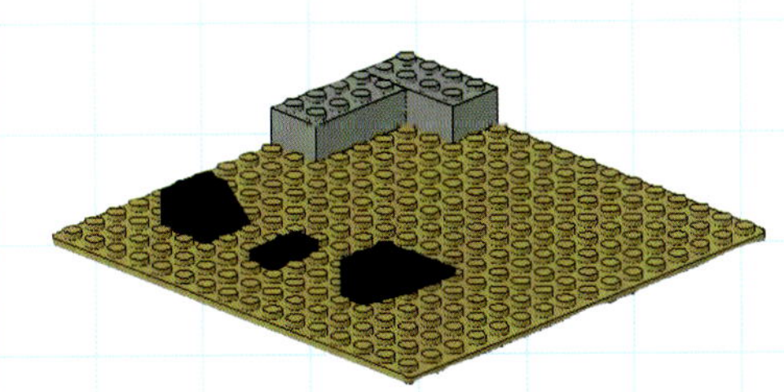

2

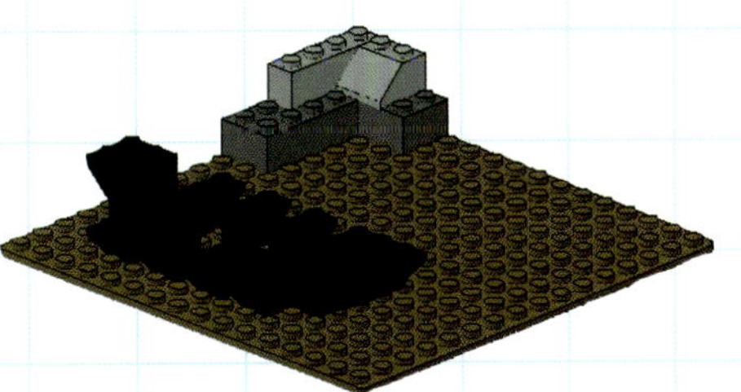

3

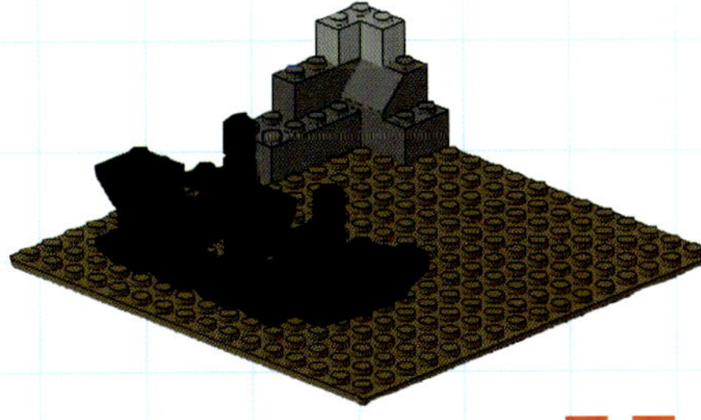

4
5
1
2
3
4
5
1
2
3
4
5
1
2
3
4

# Mini Yellow Castle

*Design and Instructions by Christopher Deck*

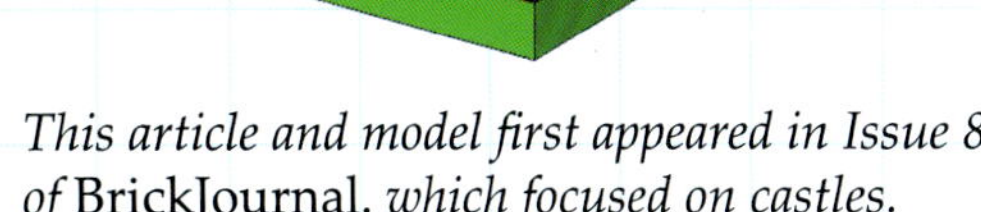

*This article and model first appeared in Issue 8 of* BrickJournal. *which focused on castles.*

Today we want to take a closer look at one of the most famous castle sets of all times! It was released more than 30 years ago in 1978 and marks the beginning of the LEGO® castle line. Today set 375 it is often just referred to as "Yellow Castle" and still is one of the most wanted castle sets.

My tribute to this legendary set is the micro version which I want to present to you now. The basis of this tiny model is 7x7 studs and thus requires a lot of jumper plates as well as a 3-piece-base plate to be centered. This is necessary to build up the many corners and edges of the castle. The piece used most for this model is the 1x1 tile with clip which is the obvious choice for the pinnacles of a micro castle.

However, the things that really make this castle unique and always recognizable are the red spots in the yellow colour scheme: The two gates and mainly the red window of the tower in the centre of the castle. The micro version features both red gates, and also the nice red window in the tower. For this we need two Technic® bricks next to each other. The rear one has an axle hole and holds a 2-wide red axle while the front one has a standard hole which leaves some empty space around the axle. This creates the illusion of a red window frame.

With that I think we're done and have a finished micro building. I wish you happy building!

## Parts List

| Qty. | Part | Description | Color |
|---|---|---|---|
| 1 | 4490.dat | Arch 1 x 3 | Yellow |
| 1 | 3659.dat | Arch 1 x 4 | Yellow |
| 4 | 3005.dat | Brick 1 x 1 | Yellow |
| 6 | 4070.dat | Brick 1 x 1 with Headlight | Yellow |
| 2 | 3003.dat | Brick 2 x 2 | Yellow |
| 4 | 6188.dat | Cone 1 x 1 | Yellow |
| 2 | 30002.dat | Minifig Goblet | Yellow |
| 2 | 3024.dat | Plate 1 x 1 | Yellow |
| 1 | 3023.dat | Plate 1 x 2 | Yellow |
| 9 | 3794.dat | Plate 1 x 2 with 1 Stud | Yellow |
| 1 | 4477.dat | Plate 1 x 10 | Bright Green |
| 2 | 3022.dat | Plate 2 x 2 | Yellow |
| 3 | 4032.dat | Plate 2 x 2 Round | Yellow |
| 2 | 3030.dat | Plate 4 x 10 | Bright Green |
| 1 | 32062.dat | Technic Axle 2 Notched | Red |
| 3 | 32064.dat | Technic Brick 1 x 2 with Axlehole | Yellow |
| 1 | 3700.dat | Technic Brick 1 x 2 with Hole | Yellow |
| 23 | 2555.dat | Tile 1 x 1 with Clip | Yellow |
| 2 | 3070b.dat | Tile 1 x 1 with Groove | Yellow |
| 1 | 3069b.dat | Tile 1 x 2 with Groove | Red |
| 1 | 3068b.dat | Tile 2 x 2 with Groove | Red |

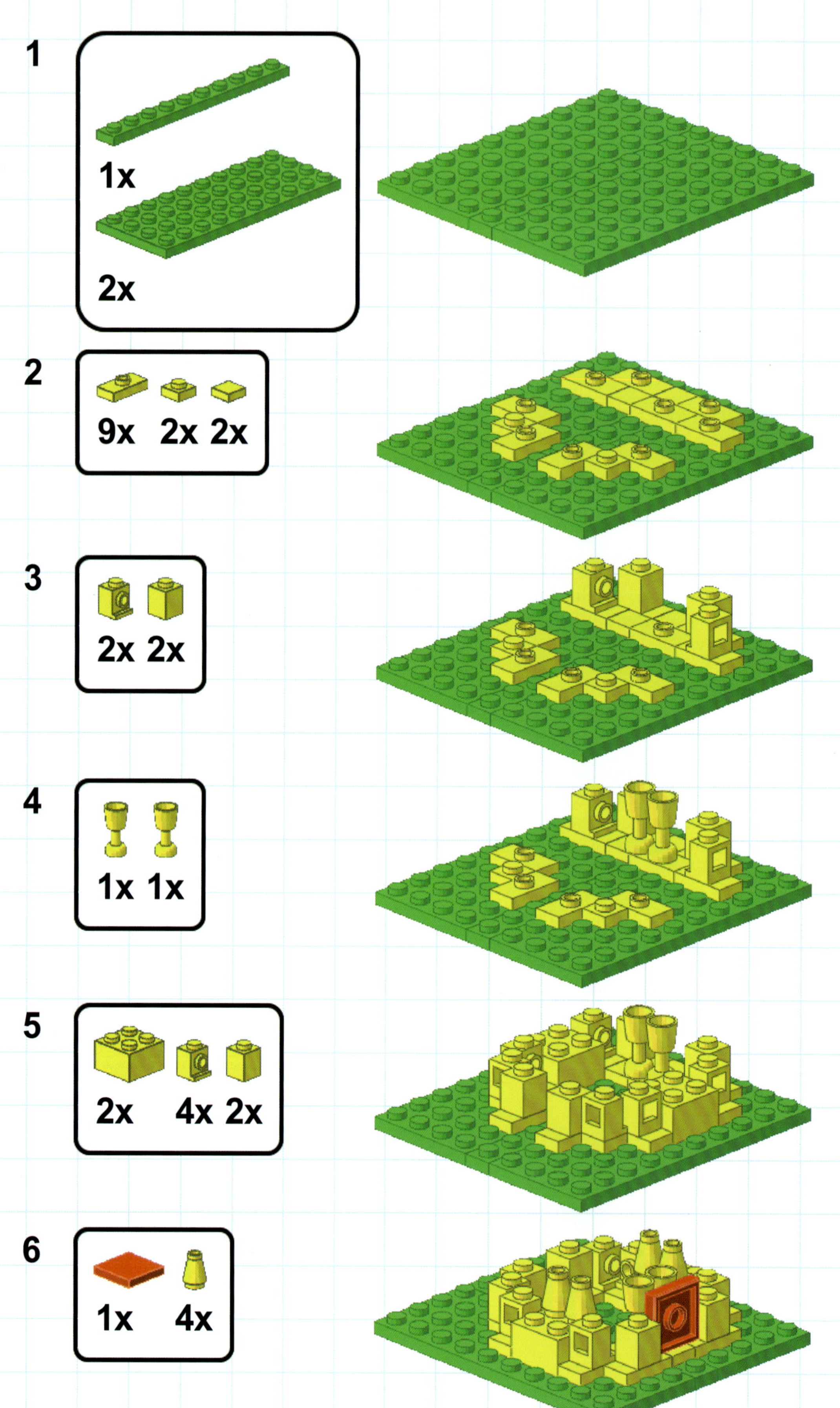
1
1x
2x
2
9x 2x 2x
3
2x 2x
4
1x 1x
5
2x 4x 2x
6
1x 4x

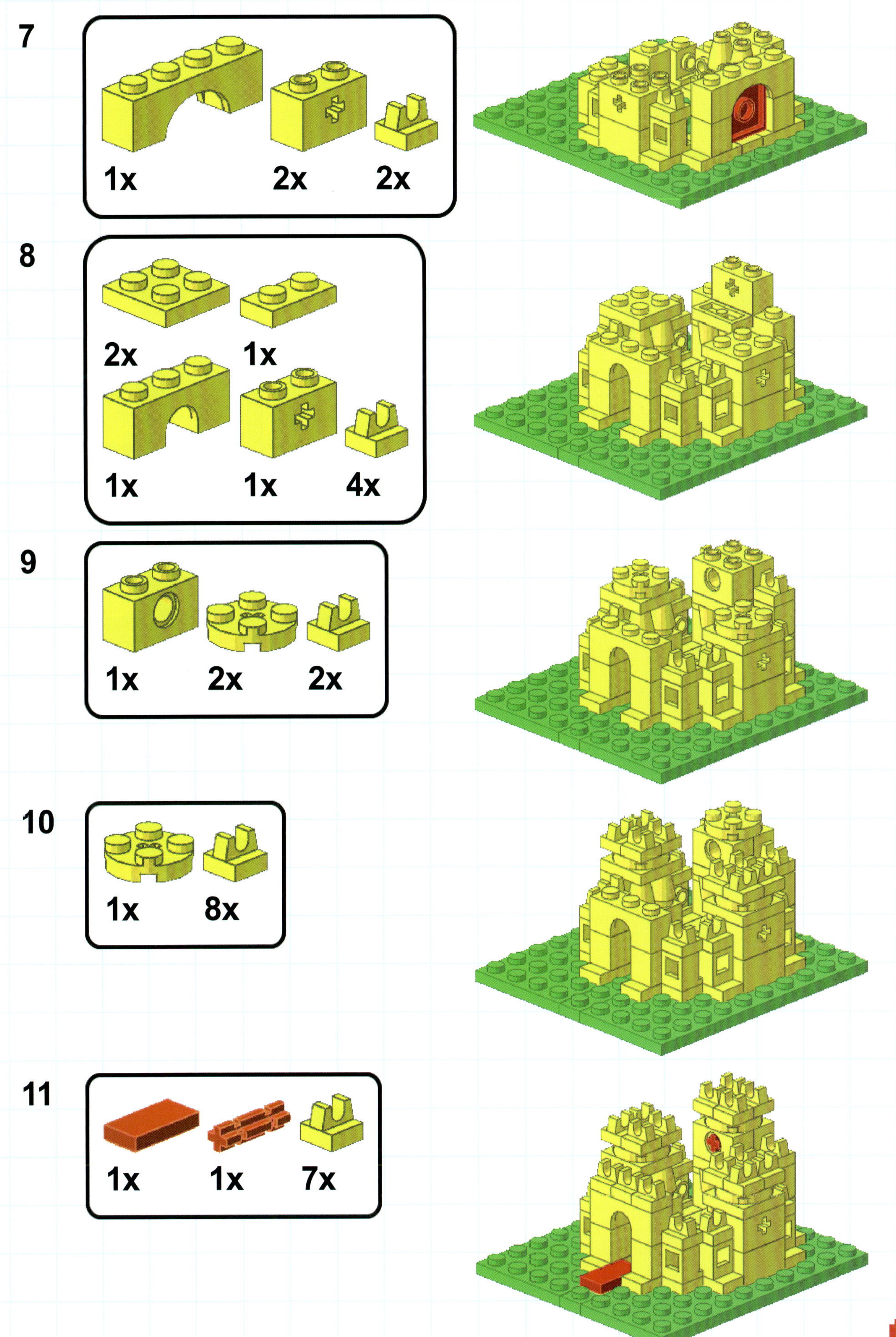

7
1x
2x
2x
8
2x
1x
1x
1x
4x
9
1x
2x
2x
10
1x
8x
11
1x
1x
7x

# The Seven Seas Will Never be the Same!

*Design by Allan Bedford*

*This article and model first appeared in Issue 2 of the online version of* BrickJournal.

What happens when you take a classic LEGO set, shrink it by half and give it an up-to-date color scheme? You end up with the Mini Constellation, of course! I've always been a fan of the set #398, the *U.S.S. Constellation,* but the official set is much too big to sit on top of my computer monitor. To get around that problem, I built a scaled-down version using colors taken from the actual ship following its restoration in the late 1990s. The result is a mini-version of the ship that easily fits on a computer monitor or a small shelf.

# Parts List

| Qty | Part | Description | Color |
|---|---|---|---|
| 3 | 2420.dat | Plate 2 x 2 Corner | Tan |
| 2 | 2420.dat | Plate 2 x 2 Corner | Black |
| 12 | 2431.dat | Tile 1 x 4 with Groove | Black |
| 3 | 2436b.dat | Bracket 1 x 2 - 1 x 4 Type 2 | Black |
| 1 | 2555.dat | Tile 1 x 1 with Clip | Tan |
| 1 | 2555.dat | Tile 1 x 1 with Clip | Black |
| 13 | 3002.dat | Brick 2 x 3 | Blue |
| 3 | 3002.dat | Brick 2 x 3 | Black |
| 15 | 3004.dat | Brick 1 x 2 | White |
| 1 | 3004.dat | Brick 1 x 2 | Blue |
| 2 | 3004.dat | Brick 1 x 2 | Black |
| 1 | 3005.dat | Brick 1 x 1 | Blue |
| 1 | 3008.dat | Brick 1 x 8 | Red |
| 2 | 3008.dat | Brick 1 x 8 | Black |
| 4 | 3009.dat | Brick 1 x 6 | Red |
| 4 | 3009.dat | Brick 1 x 6 | Black |
| 1 | 3010.dat | Brick 1 x 4 | Red |
| 1 | 3010.dat | Brick 1 x 4 | Blue |
| 1 | 3010.dat | Brick 1 x 4 | Black |
| 4 | 3021.dat | Plate 2 x 3 | Tan |
| 2 | 3021.dat | Plate 2 x 3 | Black |
| 1 | 3022.dat | Plate 2 x 2 | Tan |
| 2 | 3022.dat | Plate 2 x 2 | White |
| 3 | 3023.dat | Plate 1 x 2 | Tan |
| 36 | 3023.dat | Plate 1 x 2 | Black |
| 5 | 3024.dat | Plate 1 x 1 | Black |
| 16 | 3040b.dat | Slope Brick 45 2 x 1 | Red |
| 20 | 3062b.dat | Brick 1 x 1 Round with Hollow Stud | Light Bluish Gray |
| 4 | 3069b.dat | Tile 1 x 2 with Groove | Black |
| 4 | 3070b.dat | Tile 1 x 1 with Groove | Black |
| 1 | 3176.dat | Plate 3 x 2 with Hole | Tan |
| 10 | 3460.dat | Plate 1 x 8 | Black |
| 3 | 3460.dat | Plate 1 x 8 | Reddish Brown |
| 4 | 3460.dat | Plate 1 x 8 | Blue |
| 3 | 3460.dat | Plate 1 x 8 | White |
| 1 | 3460.dat | Plate 1 x 8 | Brown |
| 3 | 3622.dat | Brick 1 x 3 | Black |
| 9 | 3622.dat | Brick 1 x 3 | Blue |
| 2 | 3622.dat | Brick 1 x 3 | White |
| 2 | 3622.dat | Brick 1 x 3 | Red |
| 3 | 3623.dat | Plate 1 x 3 | White |
| 1 | 3623.dat | Plate 1 x 3 | Tan |
| 11 | 3623.dat | Plate 1 x 3 | Black |
| 22 | 3660.dat | Slope Brick 45 2 x 2 Inverted | Blue |
| 5 | 3665.dat | Slope Brick 45 2 x 1 Invcrtcd | Bluc |
| 5 | 3665.dat | Slope Brick 45 2 x 1 Inverted | Black |
| 1 | 3666.dat | Plate 1 x 6 | Tan |
| 16 | 3666.dat | Plate 1 x 6 | Black |
| 4 | 3666.dat | Plate 1 x 6 | Blue |
| 10 | 3666.dat | Plate 1 x 6 | White |
| 2 | 3666.dat | Plate 1 x 6 | Red |
| 3 | 3710.dat | Plate 1 x 4 | Tan |
| 4 | 3710.dat | Plate 1 x 4 | Black |
| 1 | 3710.dat | Plate 1 x 4 | Blue |
| 3 | 3710.dat | Plate 1 x 4 | White |
| 8 | 3710.dat | Plate 1 x 4 | Red |
| 6 | 3794a.dat | Plate 1 x 2 without Groove with 1 Centre Stud | White |
| 21 | 3794b.dat | Plate 1 x 2 with Groove with 1 Centre Stud | Black |
| 20 | 4070.dat | Brick 1 x 1 with Headlight | Black |
| 2 | 4070.dat | Brick 1 x 1 with Headlight | White |
| 1 | 4287.dat | Slope Brick 33 3 x 1 Inverted | Yellow |
| 3 | 4287.dat | Slope Brick 33 3 x 1 Inverted | Blue |
| 2 | 4287.dat | Slope Brick 33 3 x 1 Inverted | Black |
| 3 | 4477.dat | Plate 1 x 10 | Reddish Brown |
| 9 | 4477.dat | Plate 1 x 10 | White |
| 2 | 6141.dat | Plate 1 x 1 Round | Red |
| 6 | 6141.dat | Plate 1 x 1 Round | White |
| 2 | 6541.dat | Technic Brick 1 x 1 with Hole | Tan |
| 2 | 6541.dat | Technic Brick 1 x 1 with Hole | Black |
| 1 | 6564.dat | Wedge 3 x 2 Right | White |
| 1 | 6564.dat | Wedge 3 x 2 Right | Black |
| 1 | 6565.dat | Wedge 3 x 2 Left | White |
| 1 | 6565.dat | Wedge 3 x 2 Left | Black |
| 4 | 6636.dat | Tile 1 x 6 | Black |
| 2 | 30039.dat | Tile 1 x 1 with Groove | Black |
| 1 | 30071.dat | Brick 1 x 1 | Black |
| 17 | 30071.dat | Brick 1 x 1 | Blue |
| 4 | 30071.dat | Brick 1 x 1 | White |
| 3 | 42446.dat | Bracket 1 x 1 - 1 x 1 | White |
| 2 | 43722.dat | Wing 2 x 3 Right | Black |
| 2 | 43723.dat | Wing 2 x 3 Left | Black |
| 1 | 44301.dat | Hinge Plate 1 x 2 Locking with Single Finger on End Vertical | White |
| 1 | 44302.dat | Hinge Plate 1 x 2 Locking with Dual Finger on End Vertical | Yellow |
| 2 | 45417.dat | Brick 2 x 2 Corner Round | Black |
| 3 | 48183.dat | Wing 3 x 4 with 1 x 2 Cutout with Stud Notches | White |
| 4 | 87087.dat | Brick 1 x 1 with Stud on 1 Side | Black |

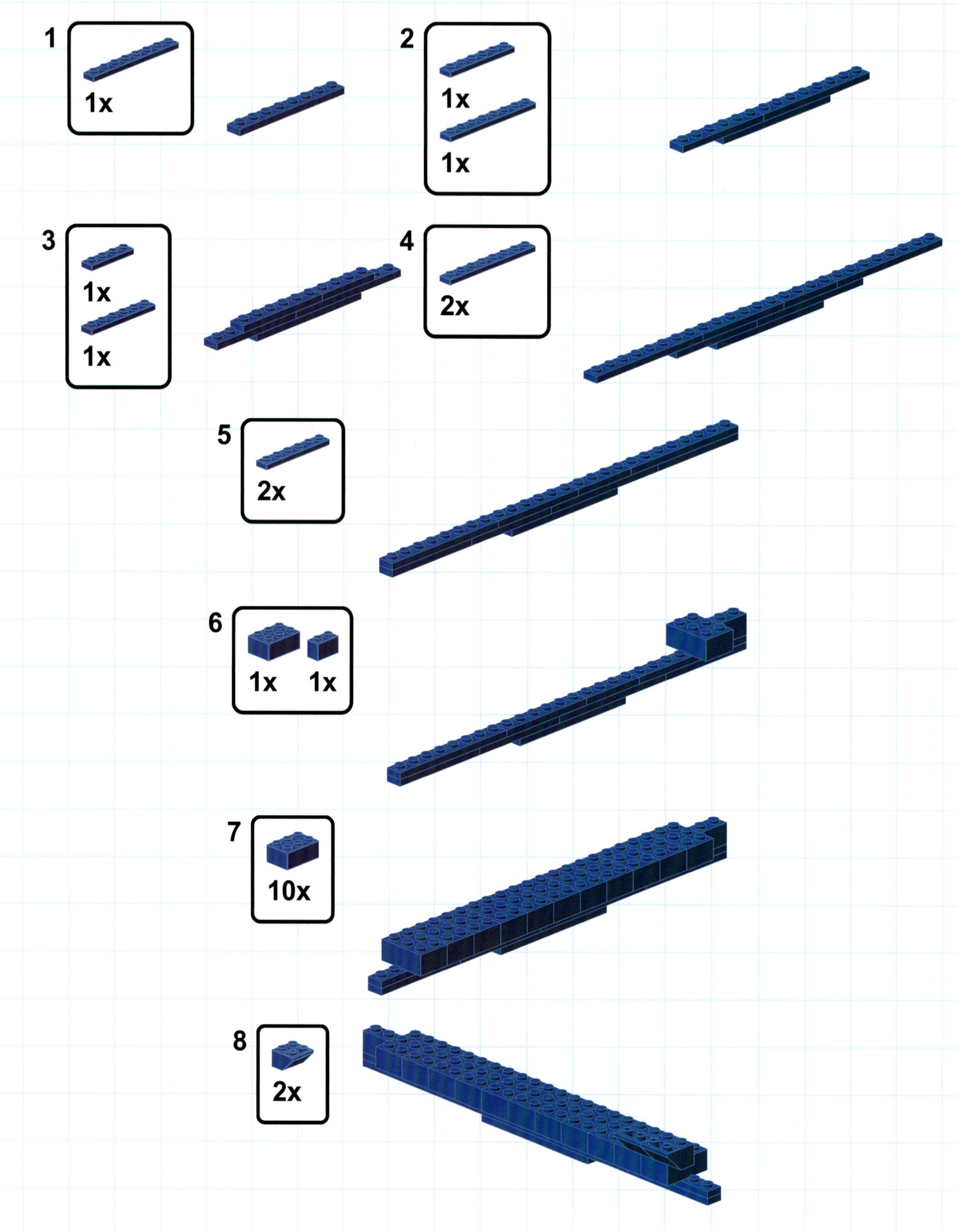
1
1x
2
1x
1x
3
1x
1x
4
2x
5
2x
6
1x
1x
7
10x
8
2x

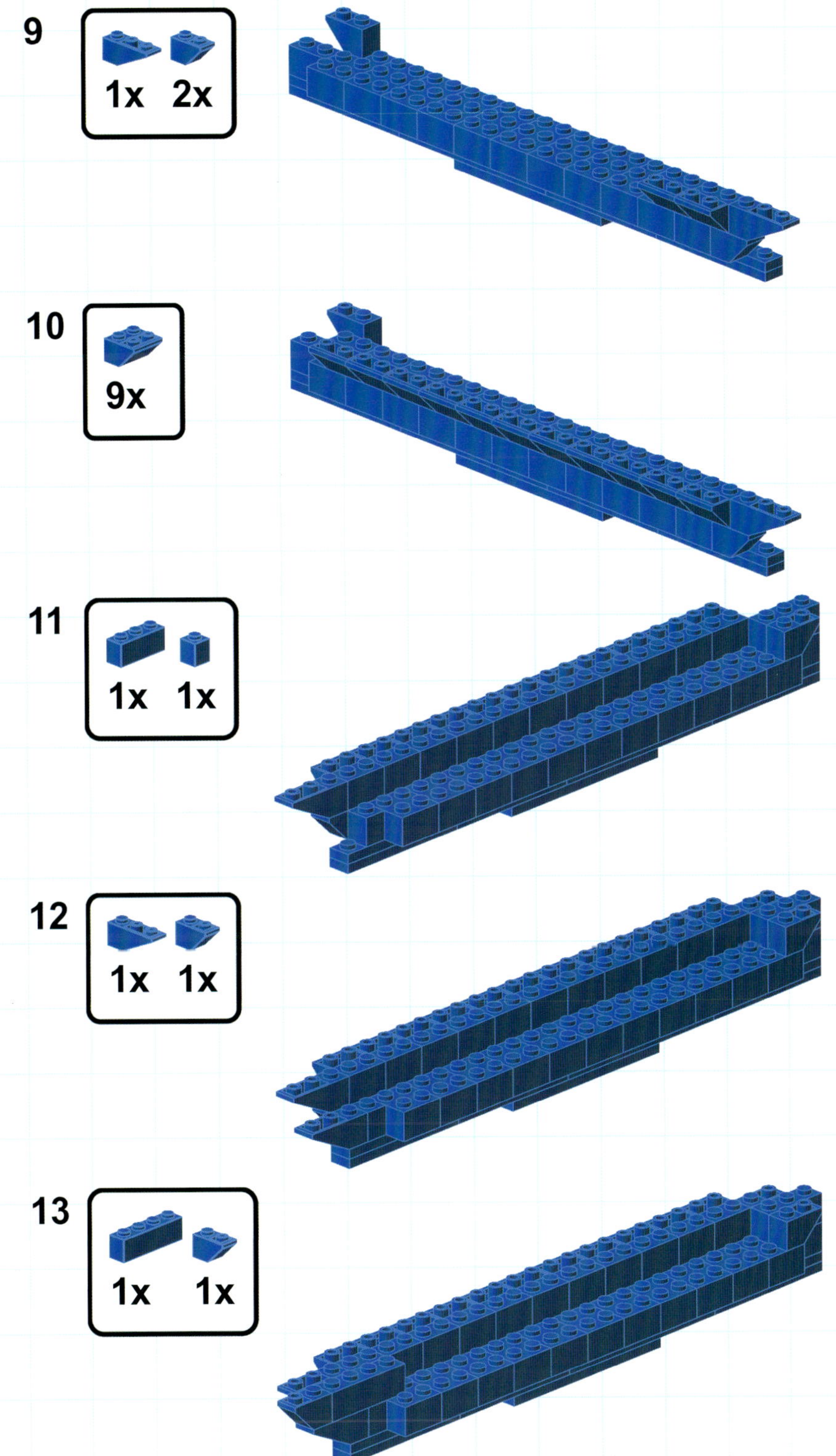
9
1x 2x
10
9x
11
1x 1x
12
1x 1x
13
1x 1x

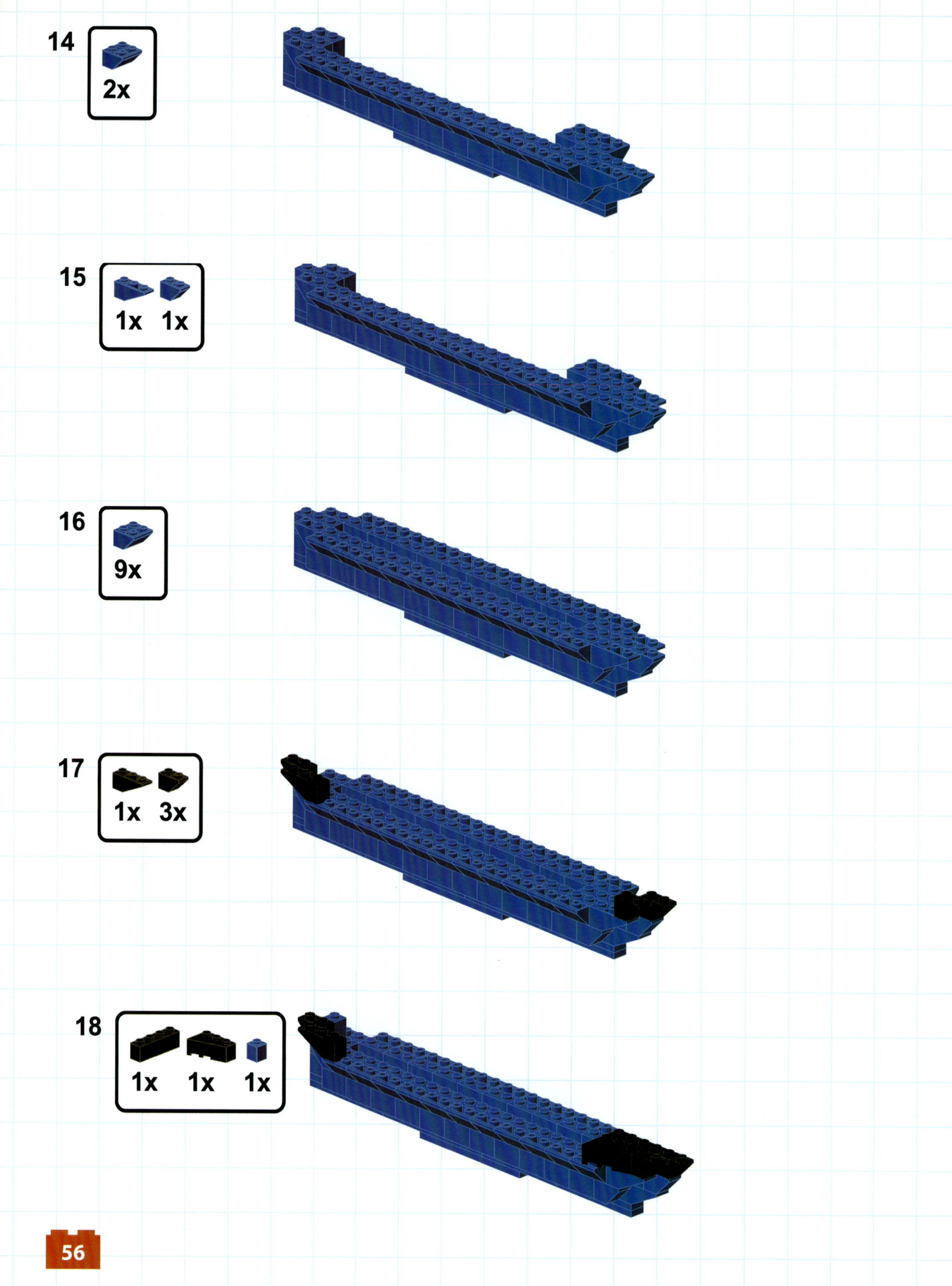
14
2x
15
1x 1x
16
9x
17
1x 3x
18
1x 1x 1x

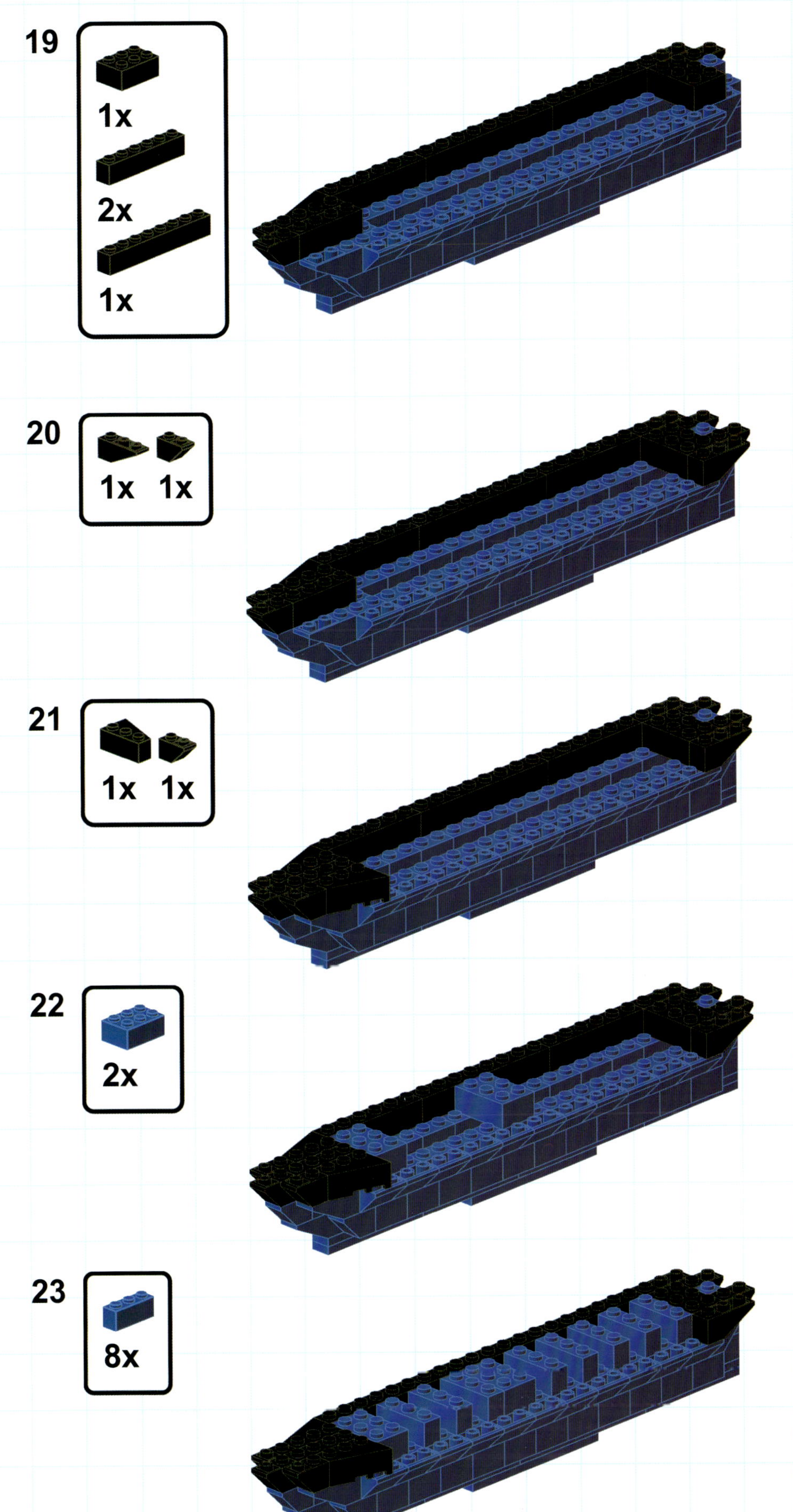
19
1x
2x
1x
20
1x 1x
21
1x 1x
22
2x
23
8x

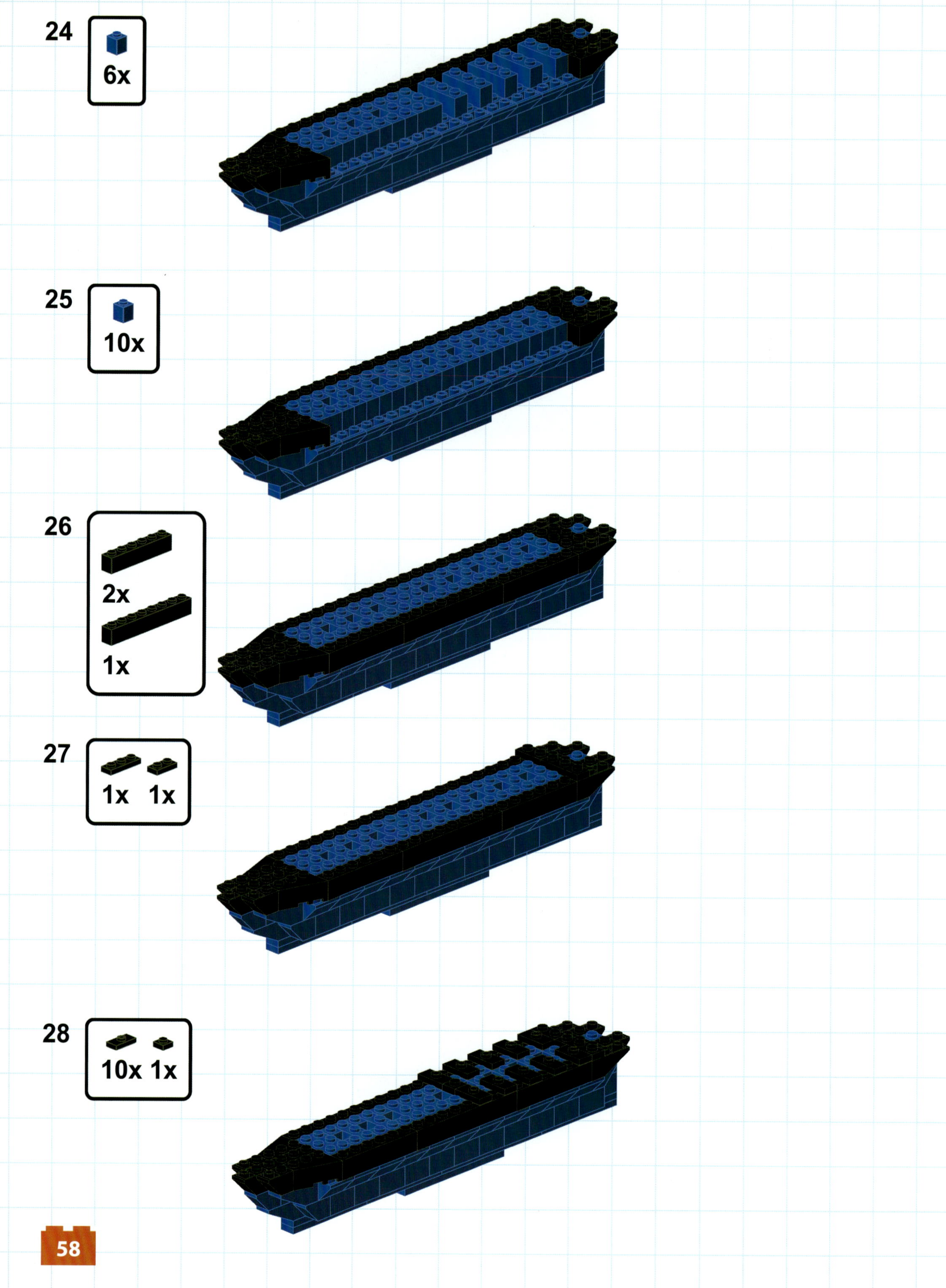
24
6x
25
10x
26
2x
1x
27
1x 1x
28
10x 1x

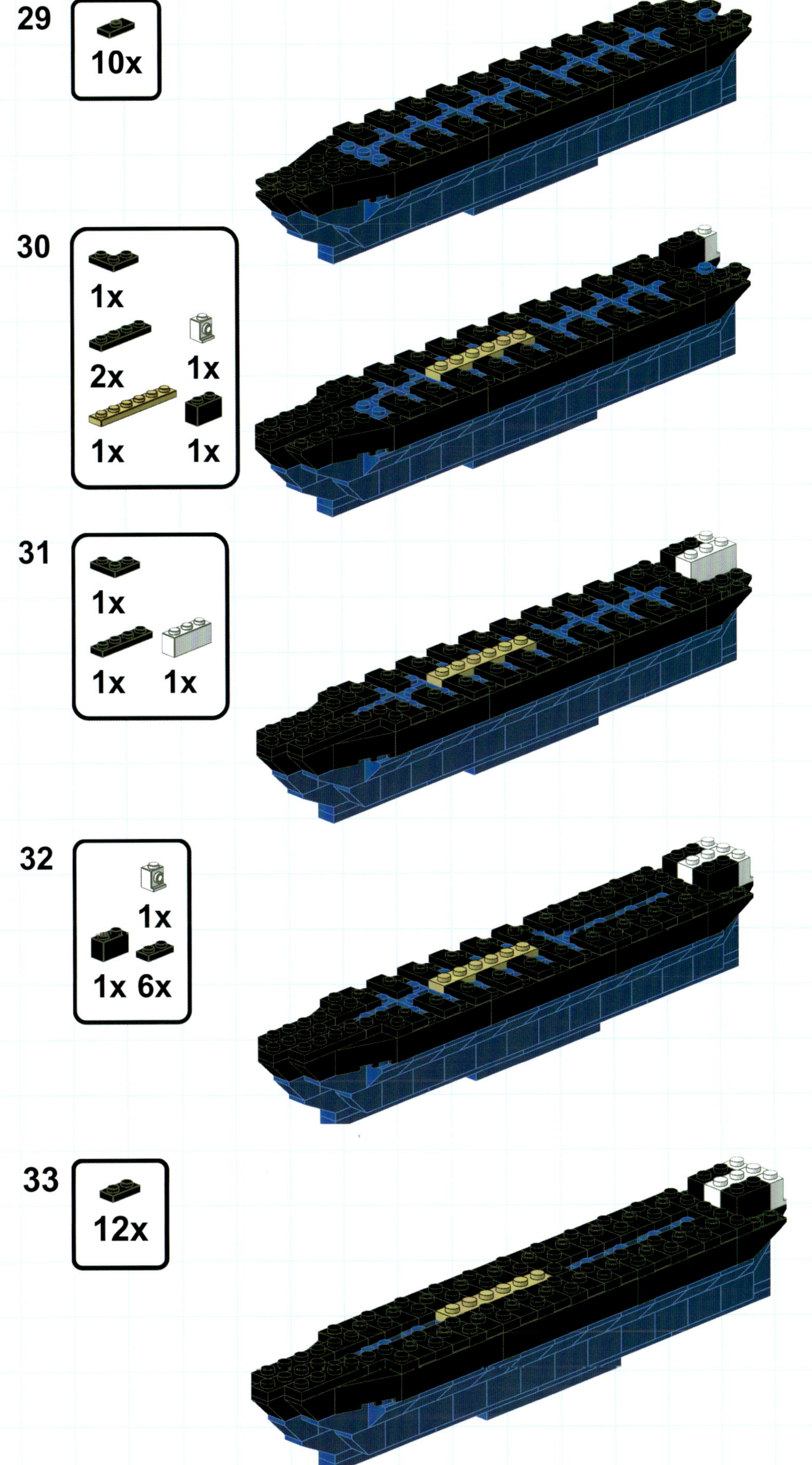
29
10x
30
1x
2x
1x
1x
1x
31
1x
1x
1x
32
1x
1x 6x
33
12x

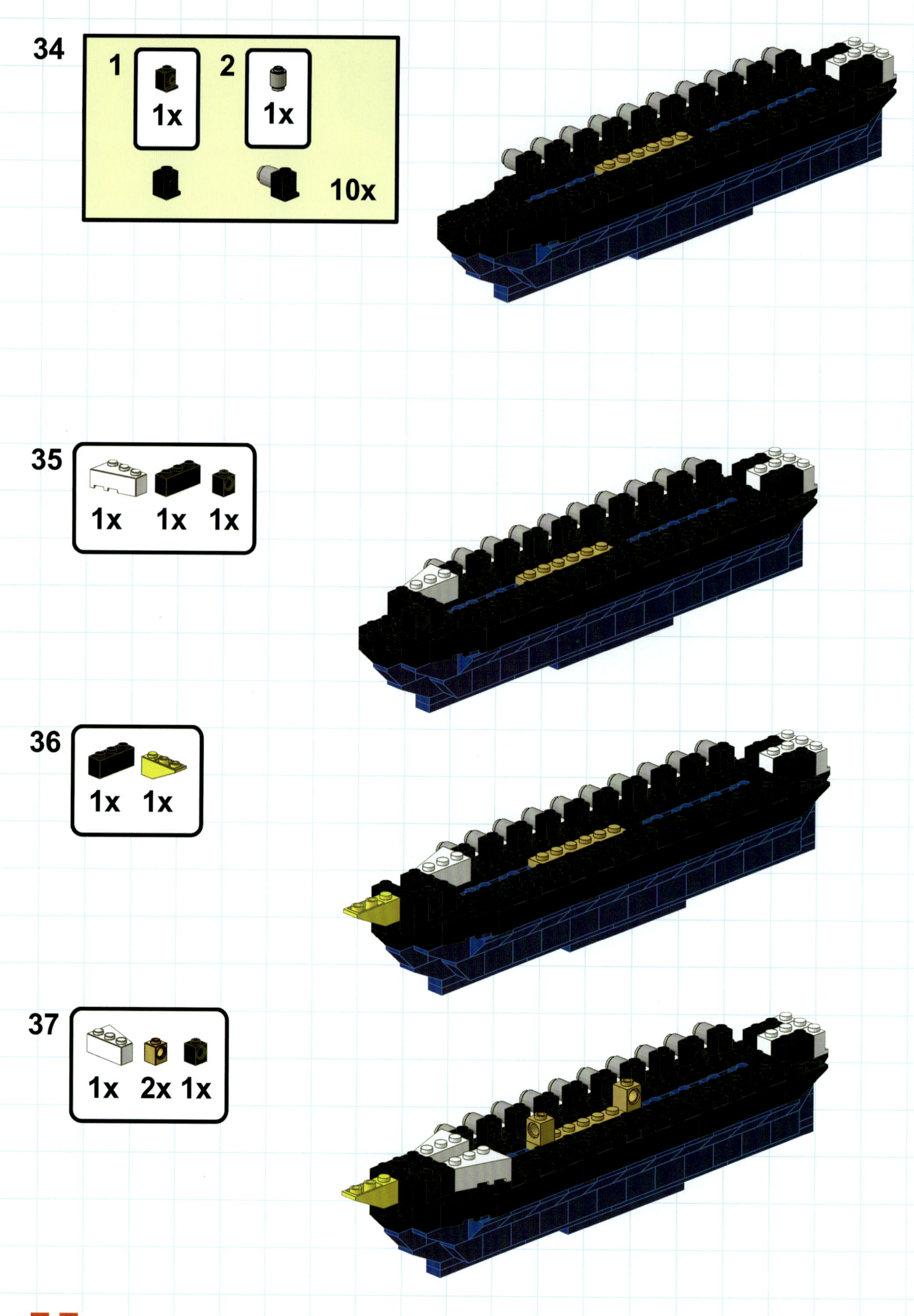

34
1
1x
2
1x
10x
35
1x 1x 1x
36
1x 1x
37
1x 2x 1x

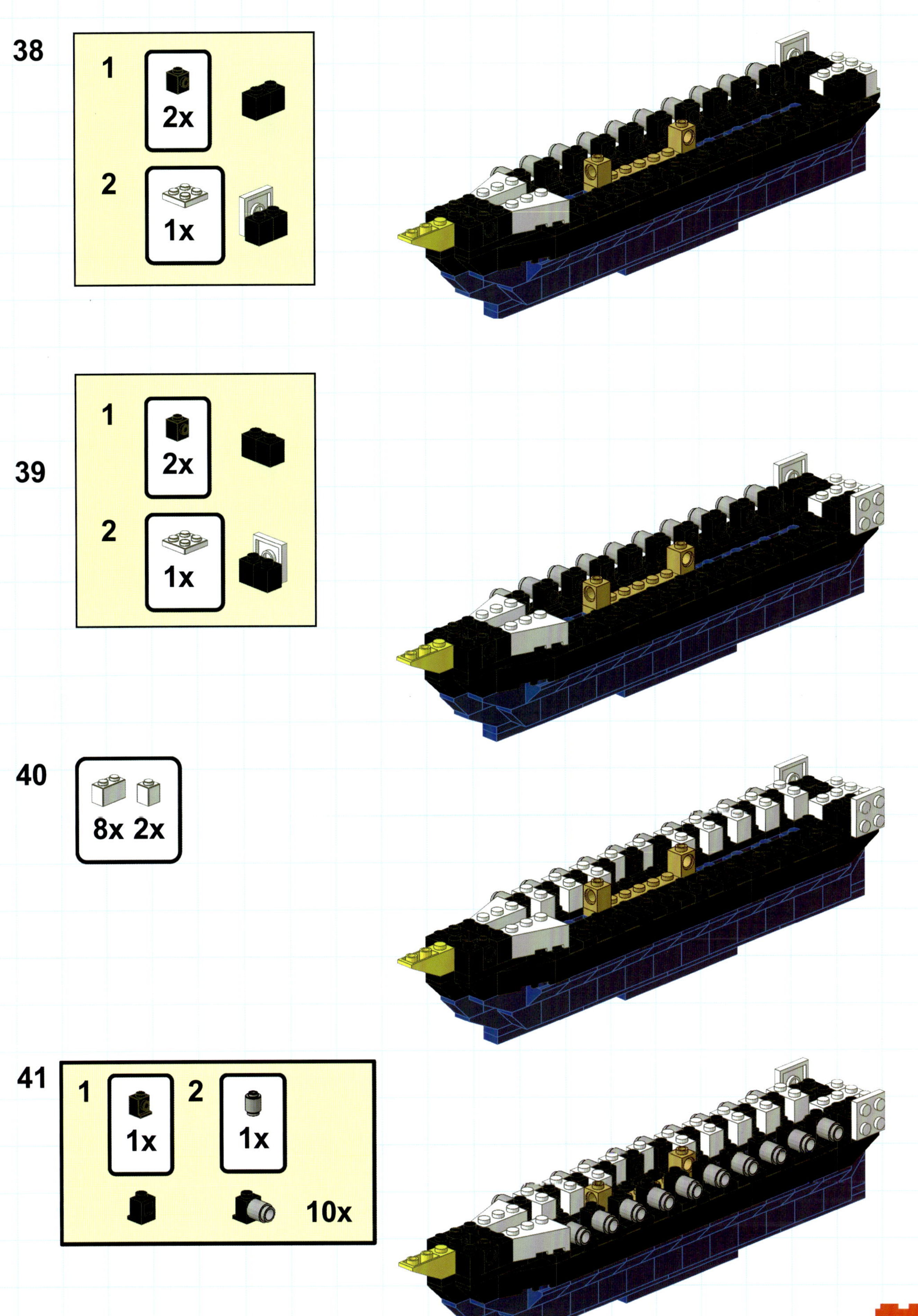

38
1
2x
2
1x
39
1
2x
2
1x
40
8x 2x
41
1
1x
2
1x
10x

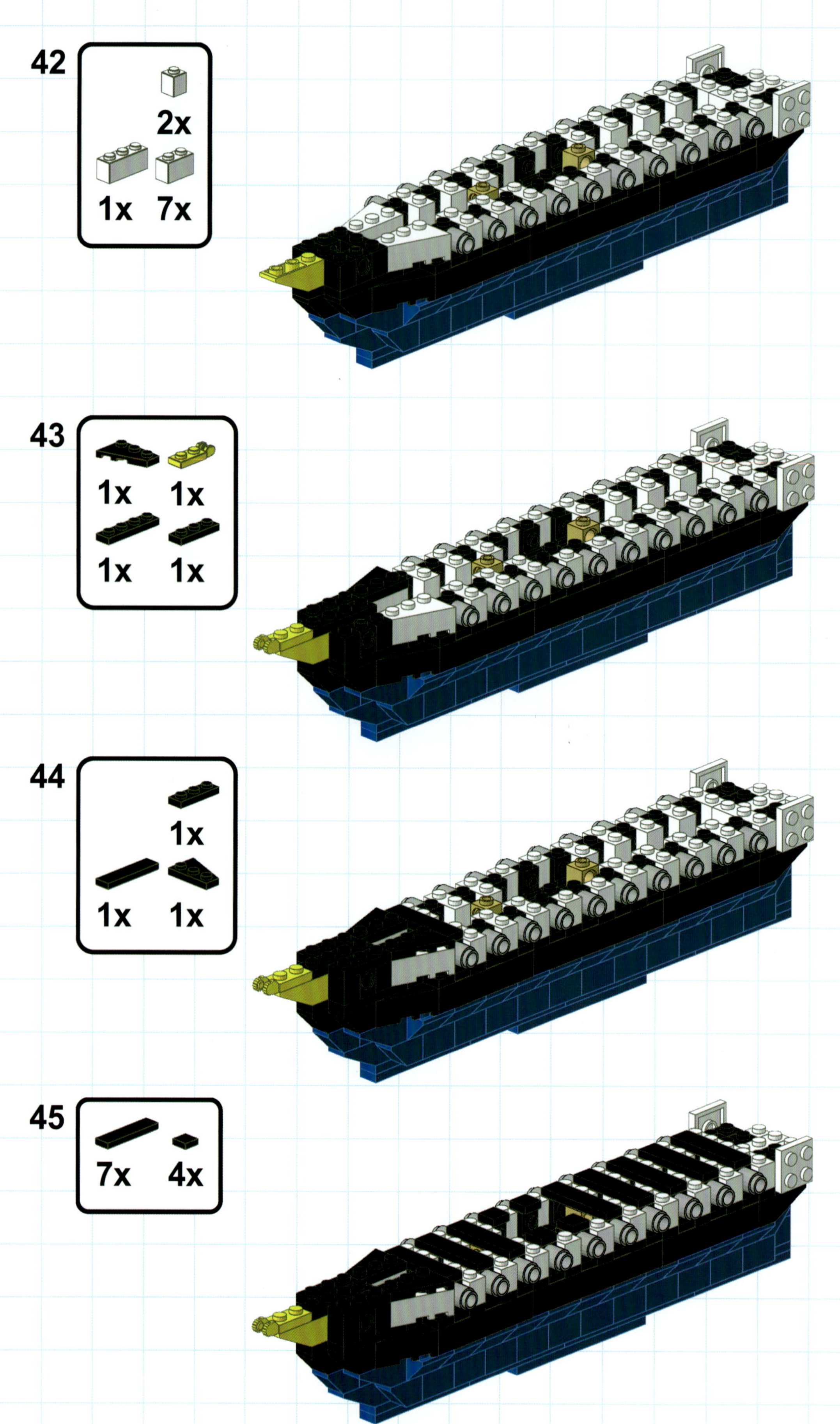
42
2x
1x 7x
43
1x 1x
1x 1x
44
1x
1x 1x
45
7x 4x

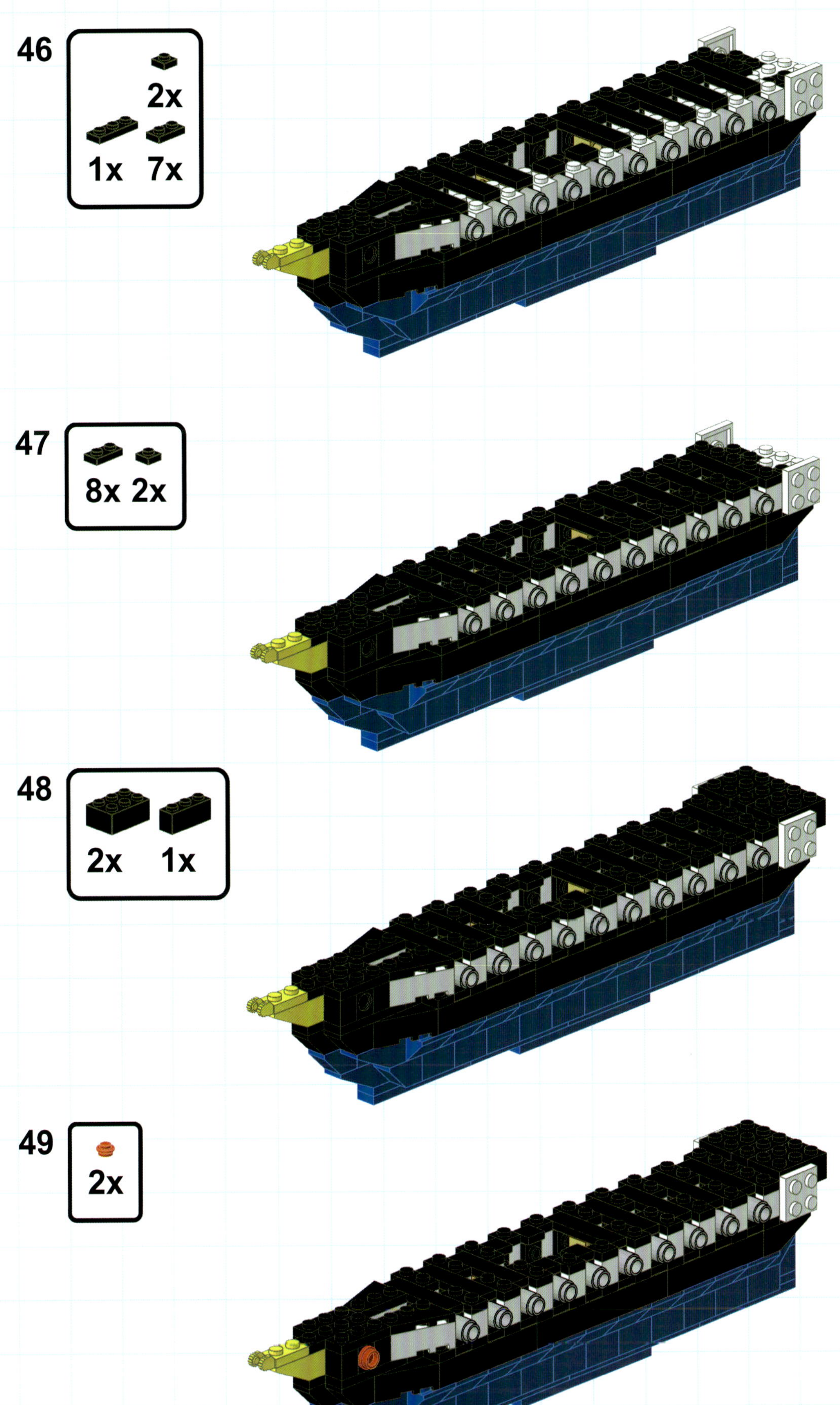
46
2x
1x 7x
47
8x 2x
48
2x 1x
49
2x

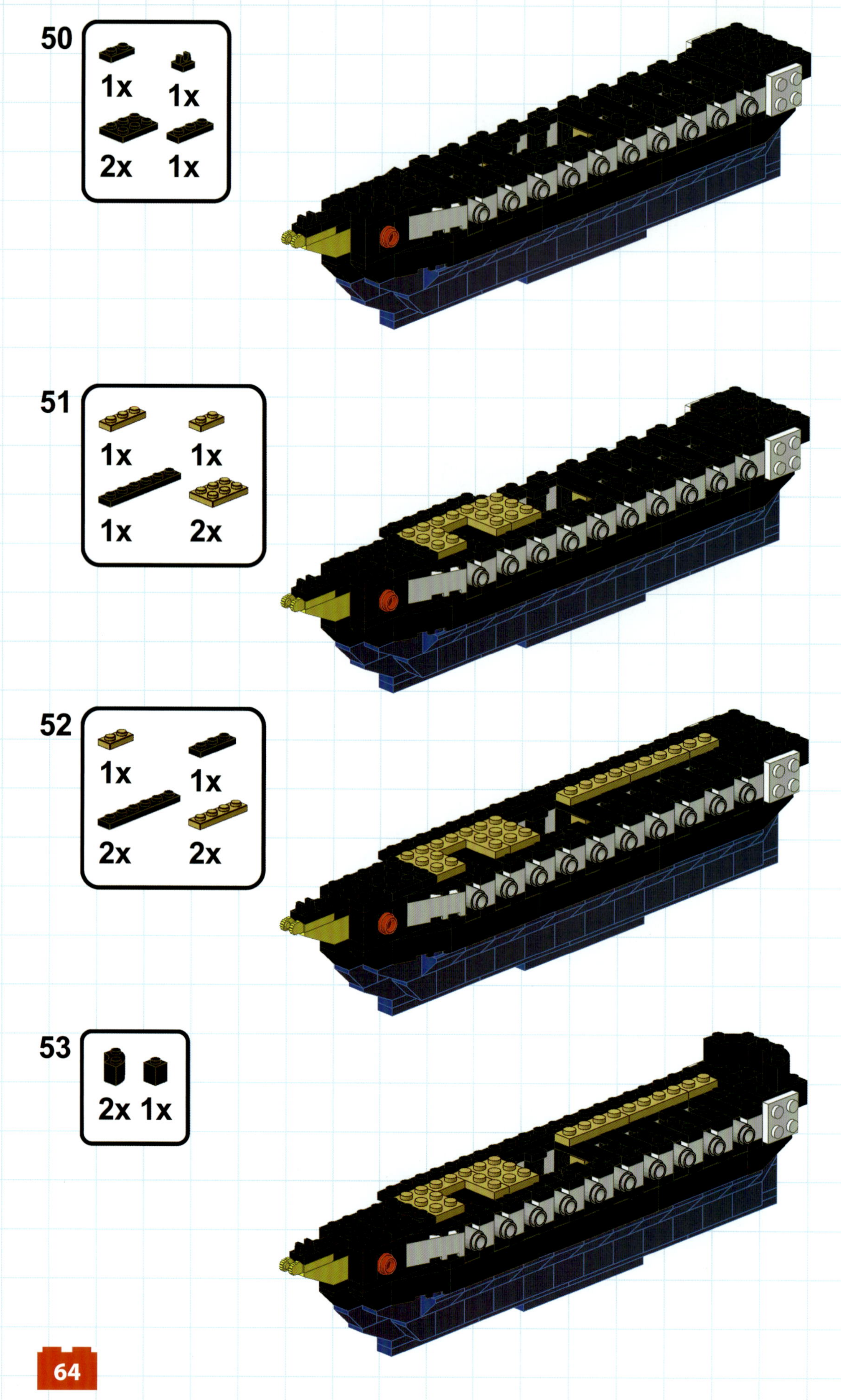
50
1x
1x
2x
1x
51
1x
1x
1x
2x
52
1x
1x
2x
2x
53
2x 1x

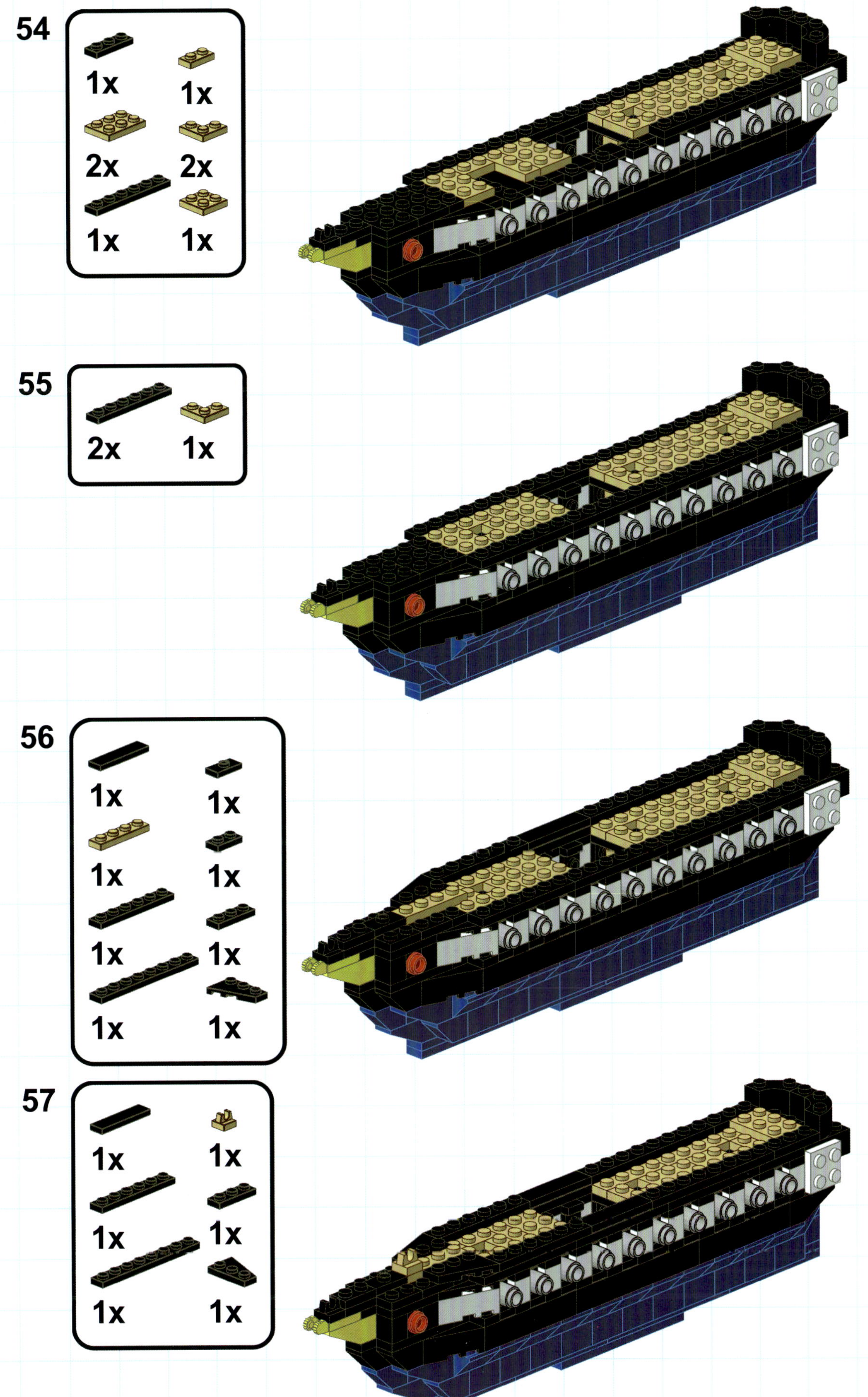
54
1x
1x
2x
2x
1x
1x
55
2x
1x
56
1x
1x
1x
1x
1x
1x
1x
1x
57
1x
1x
1x
1x
1x
1x

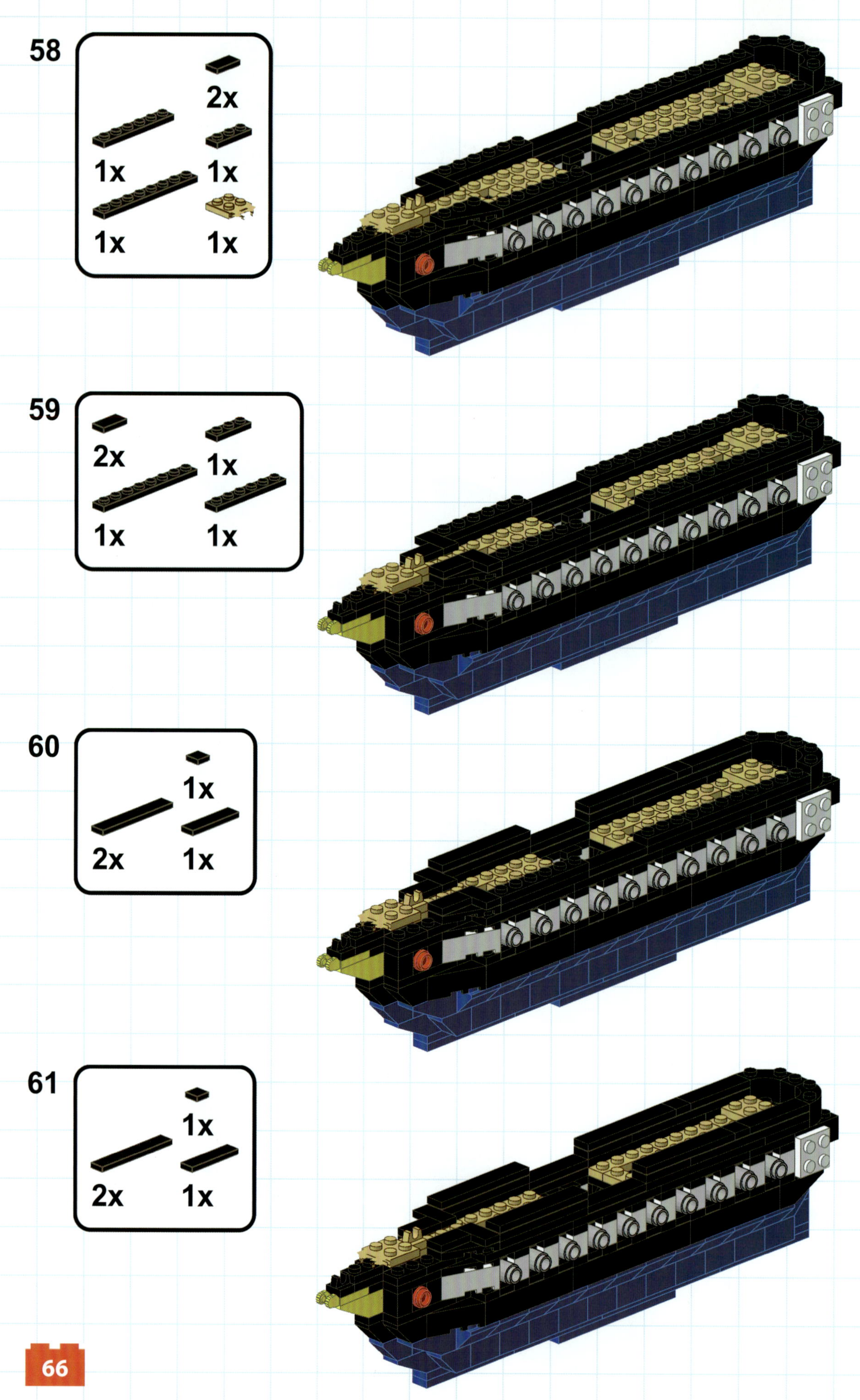
58
2x
1x
1x
1x
1x
59
2x
1x
1x
1x
60
1x
2x
1x
61
1x
2x
1x

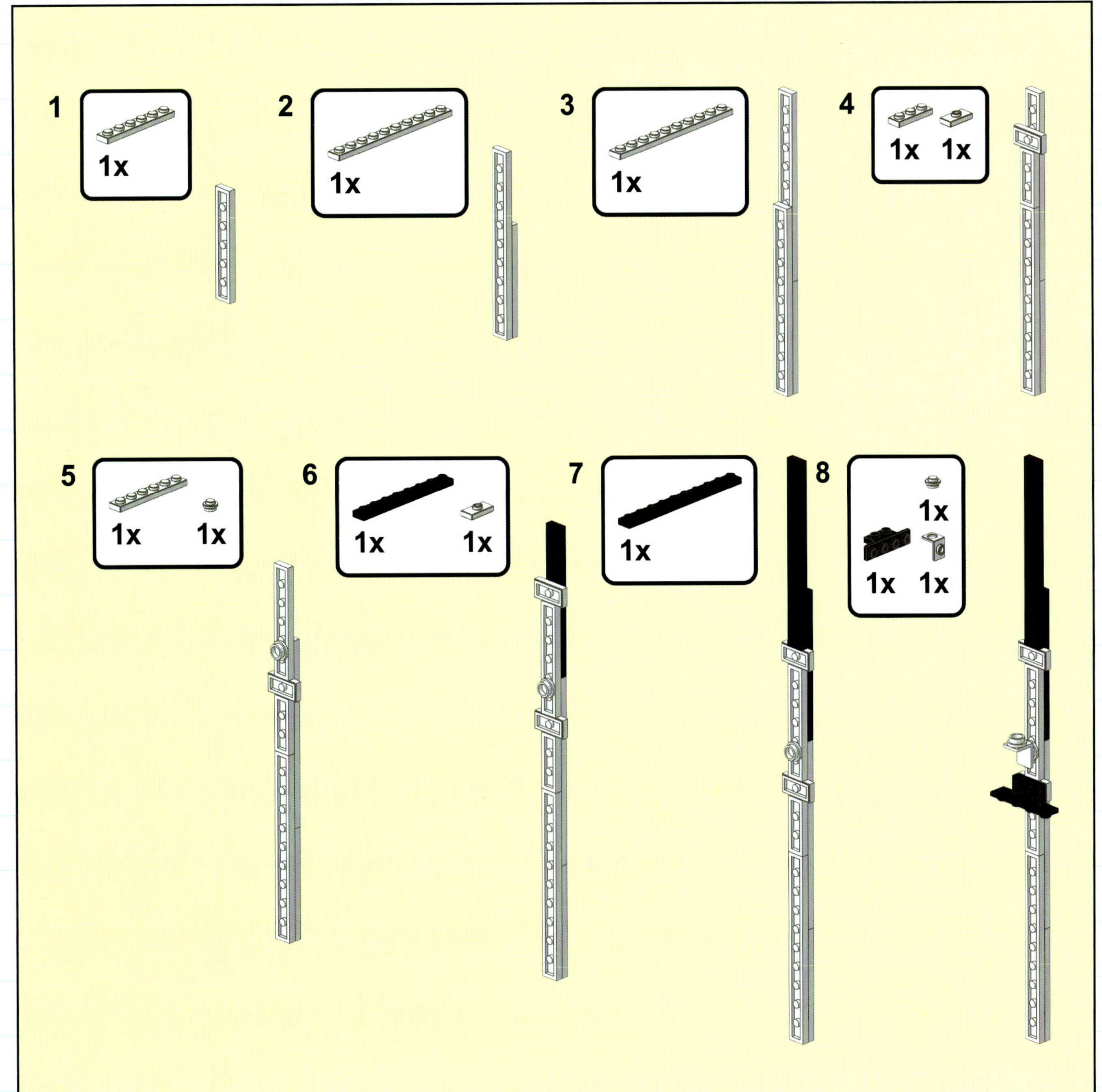
1
1x
2
1x
3
1x
4
1x 1x
5
1x 1x
6
1x 1x
7
1x
8
1x
1x 1x

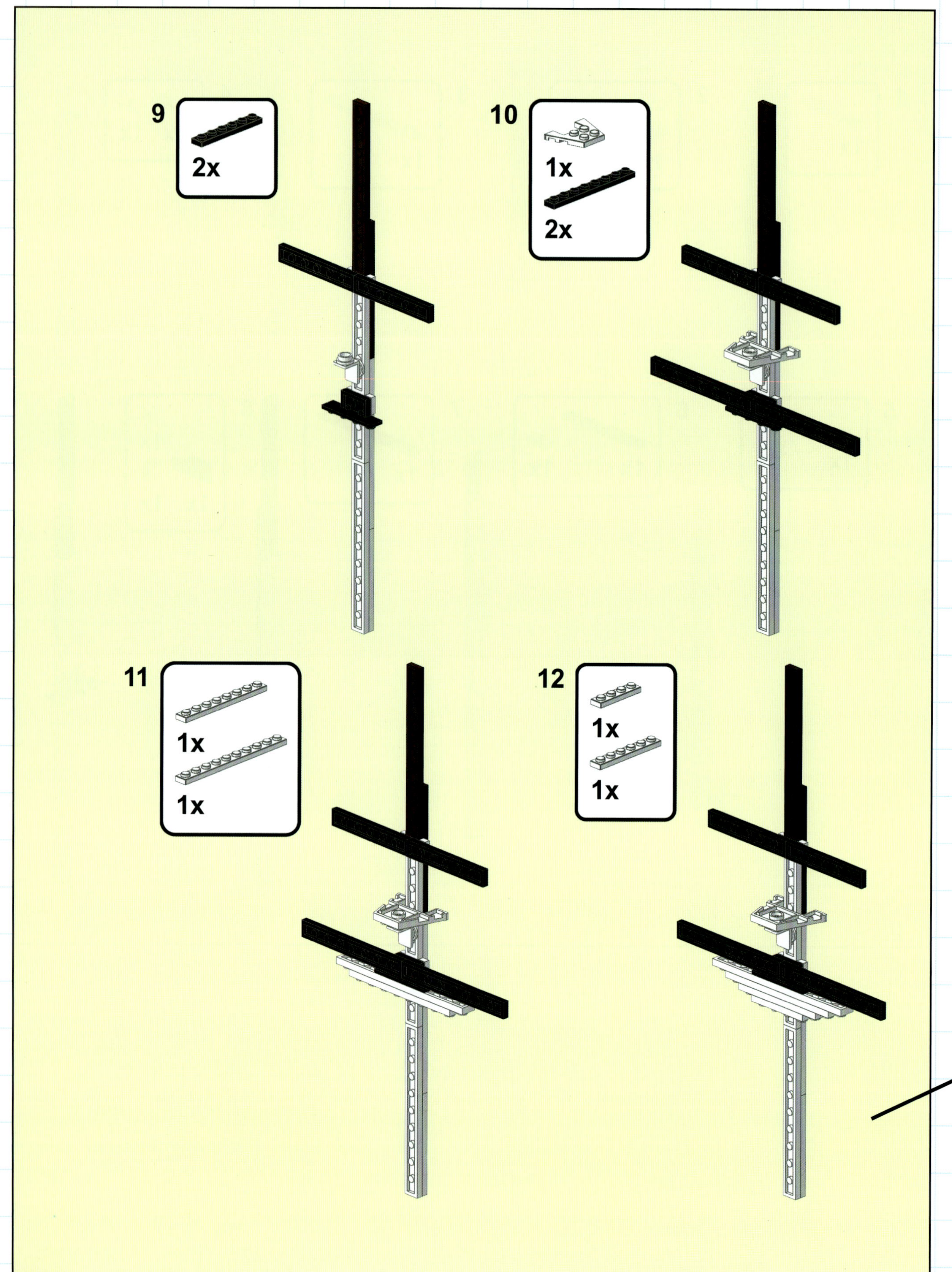
9
2x
10
1x
2x
11
1x
1x
12
1x
1x

62

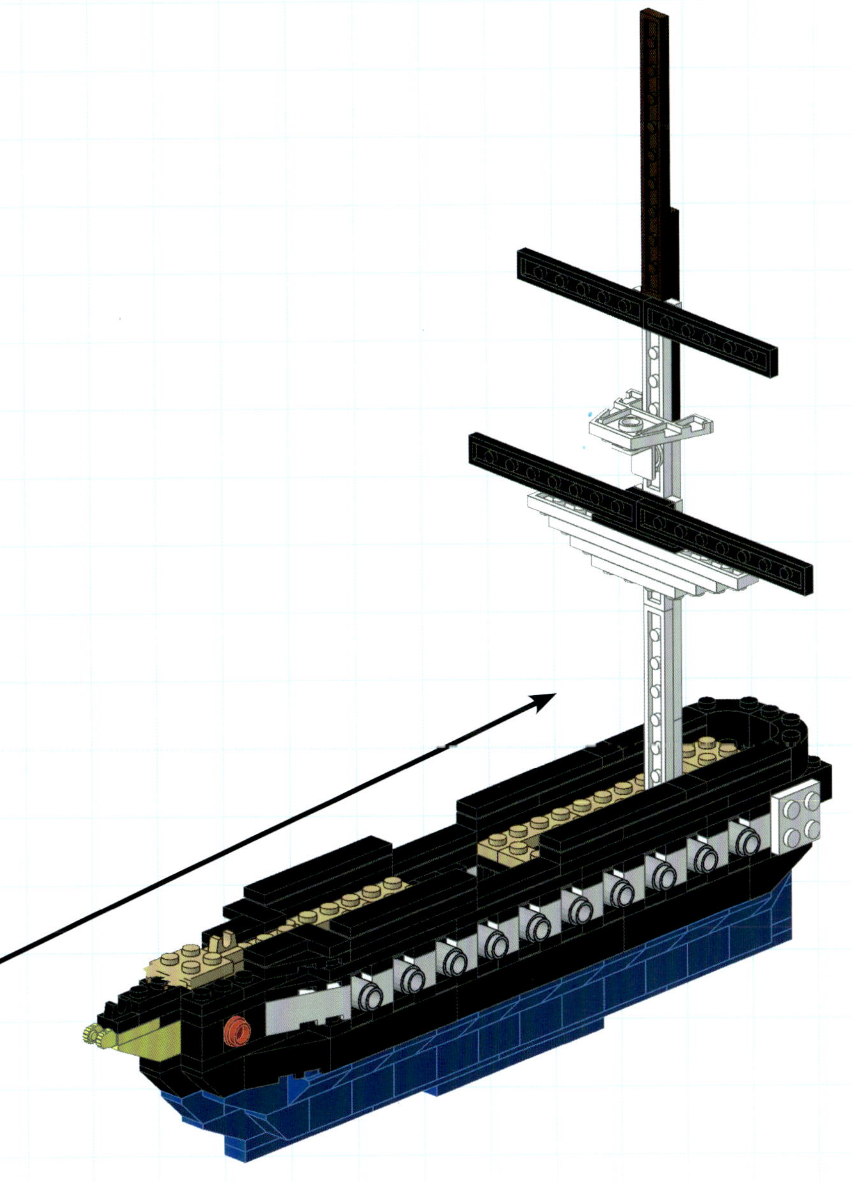

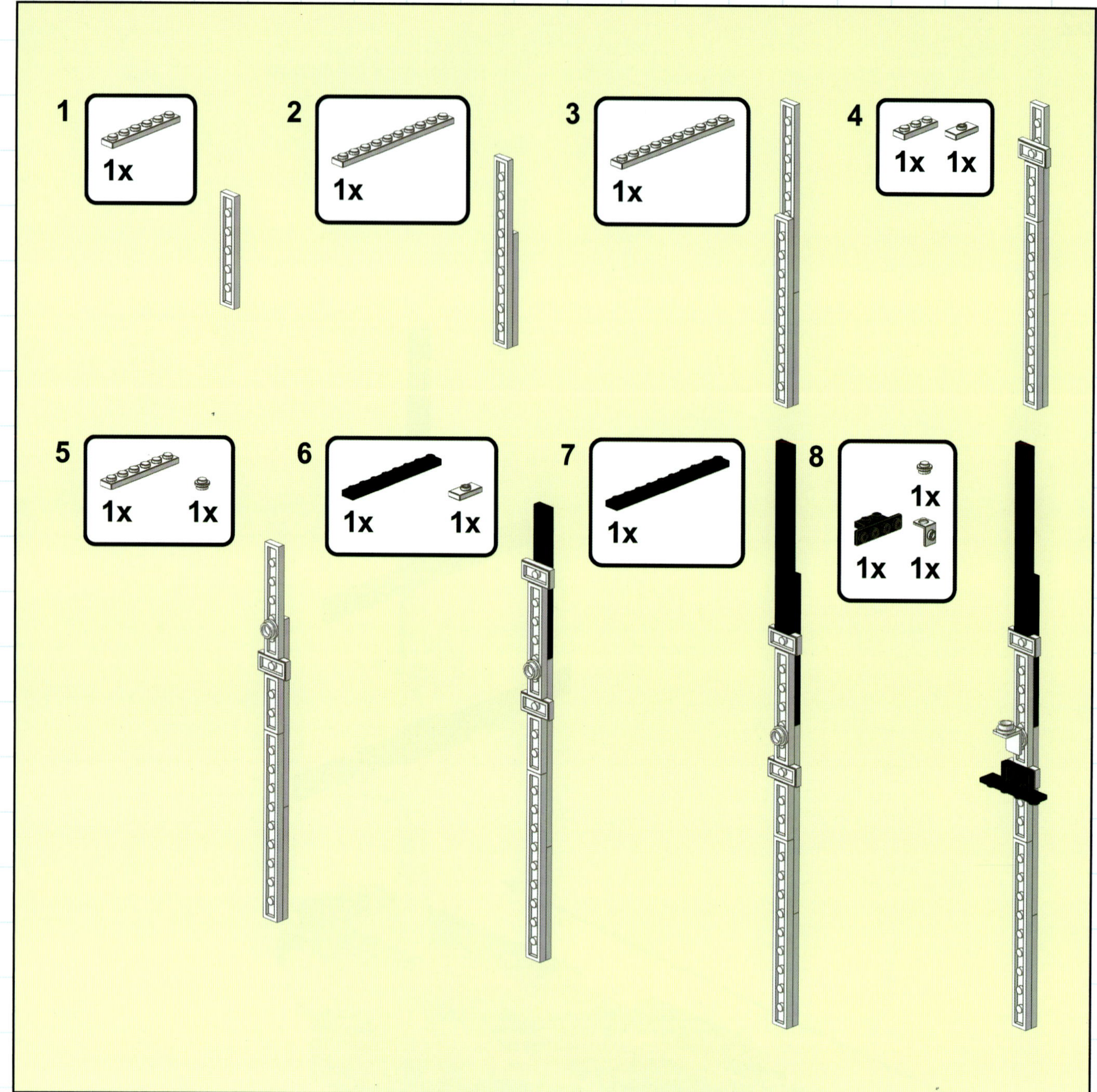
1
1x
2
1x
3
1x
4
1x 1x
5
1x 1x
6
1x 1x
7
1x
8
1x
1x 1x

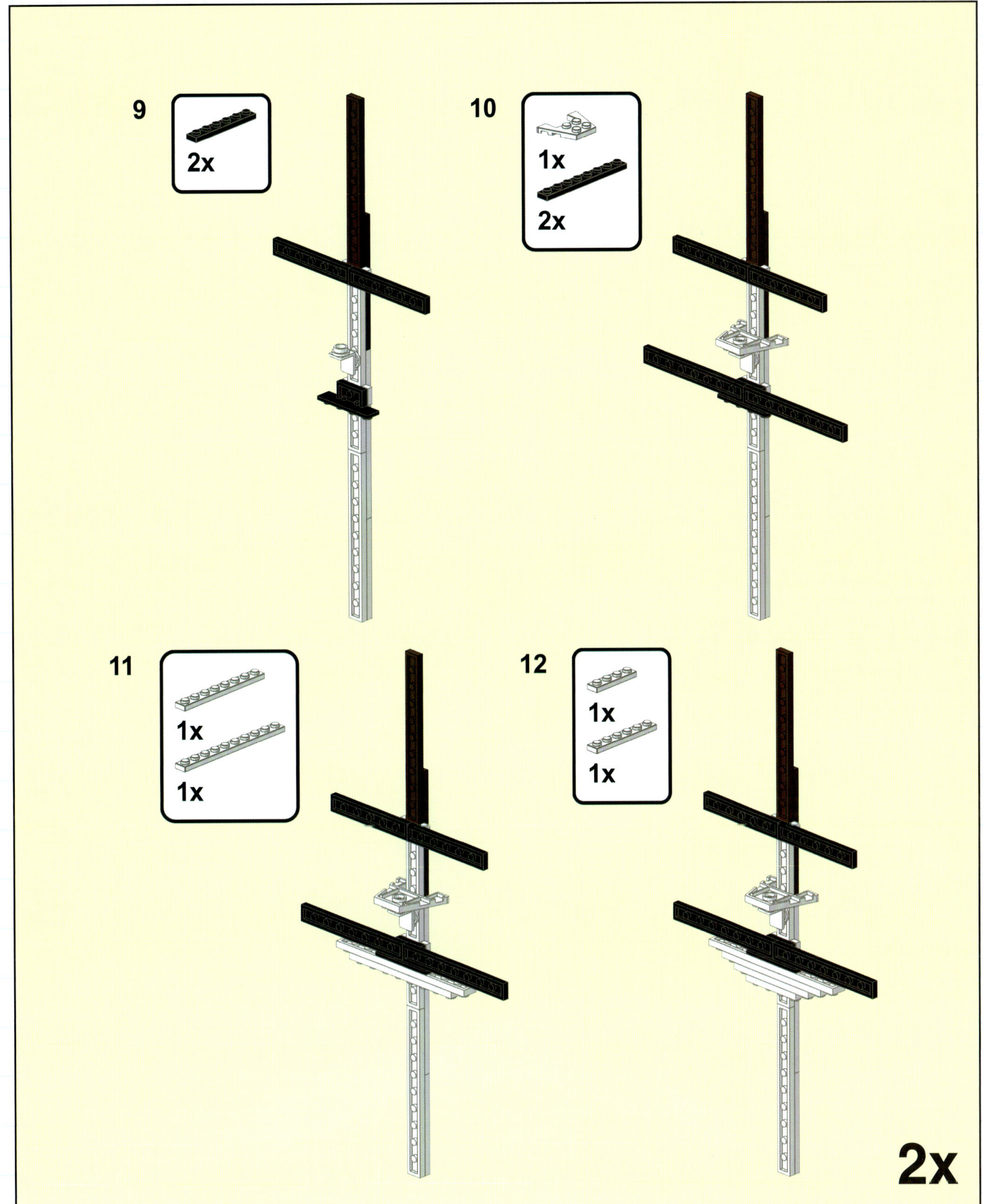
9
2x
10
1x
2x
11
1x
1x
12
1x
1x
2x

63

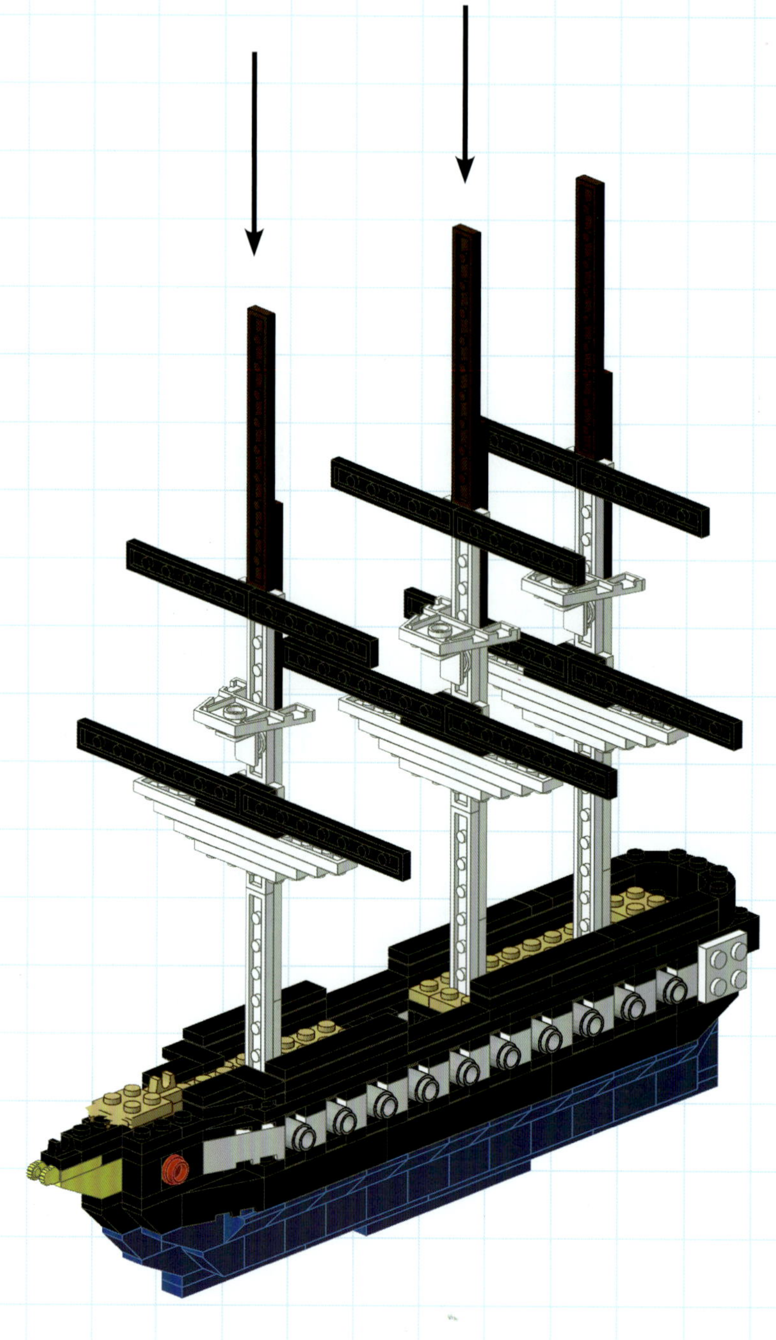

## 64

## Display Stand

1

2x

2

1x

3

2x

4

1x

5

1x

6

2x

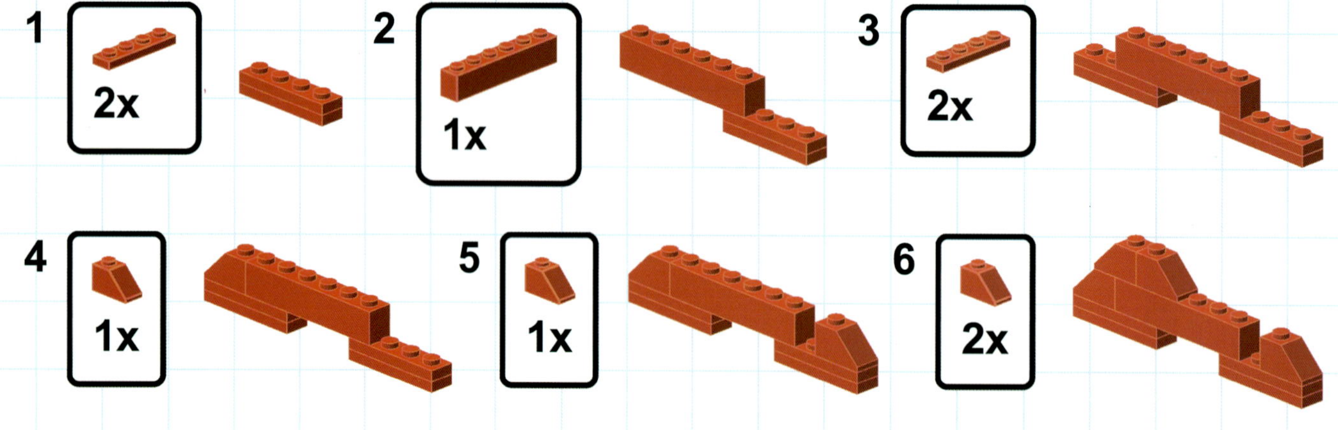

7

1
1x
2
1x
3
1x
4
1x
1x

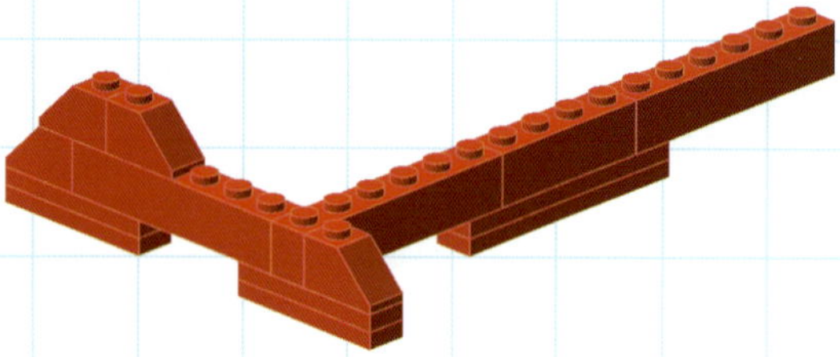

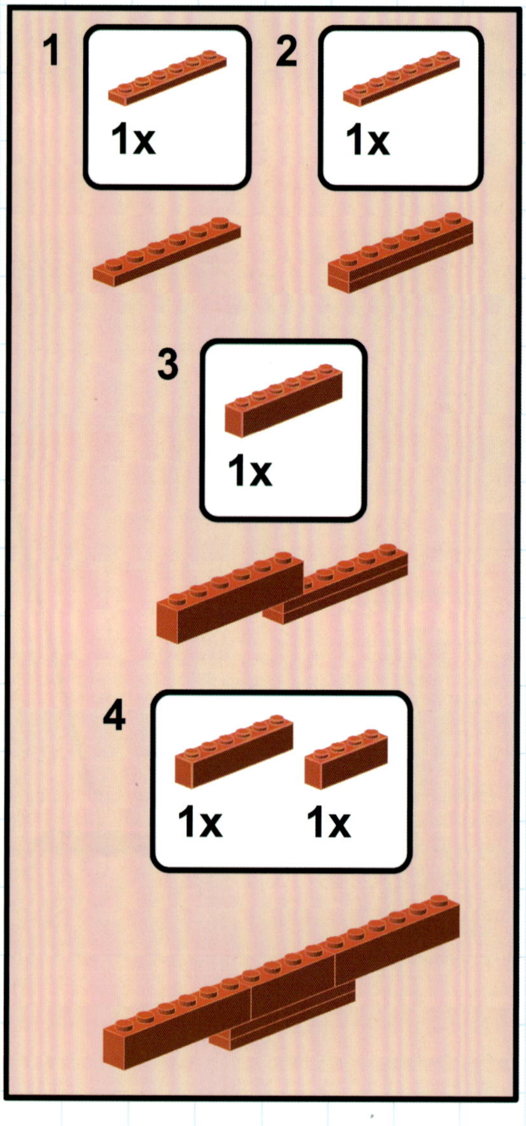

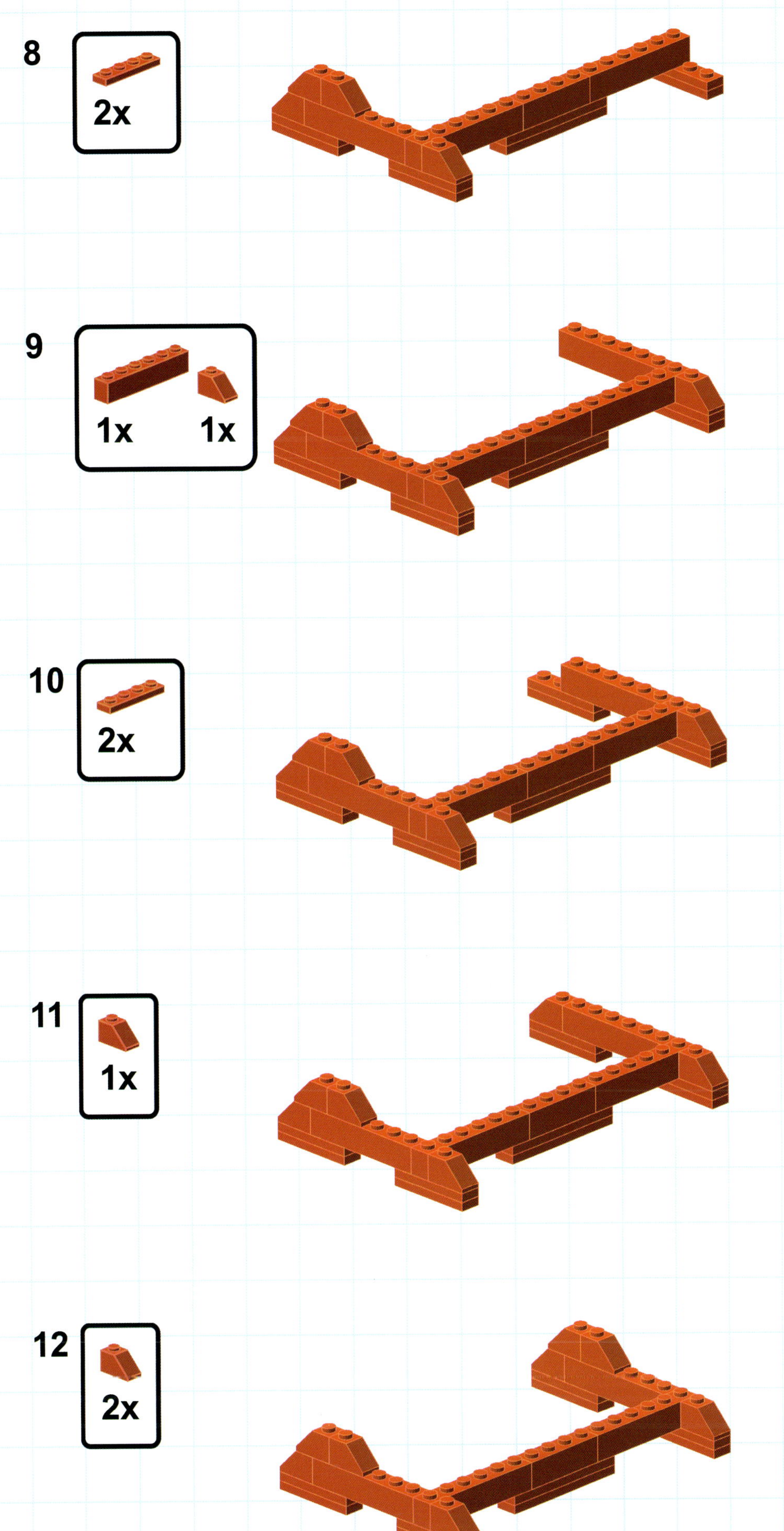
8
2x
9
1x
1x
10
2x
11
1x
12
2x

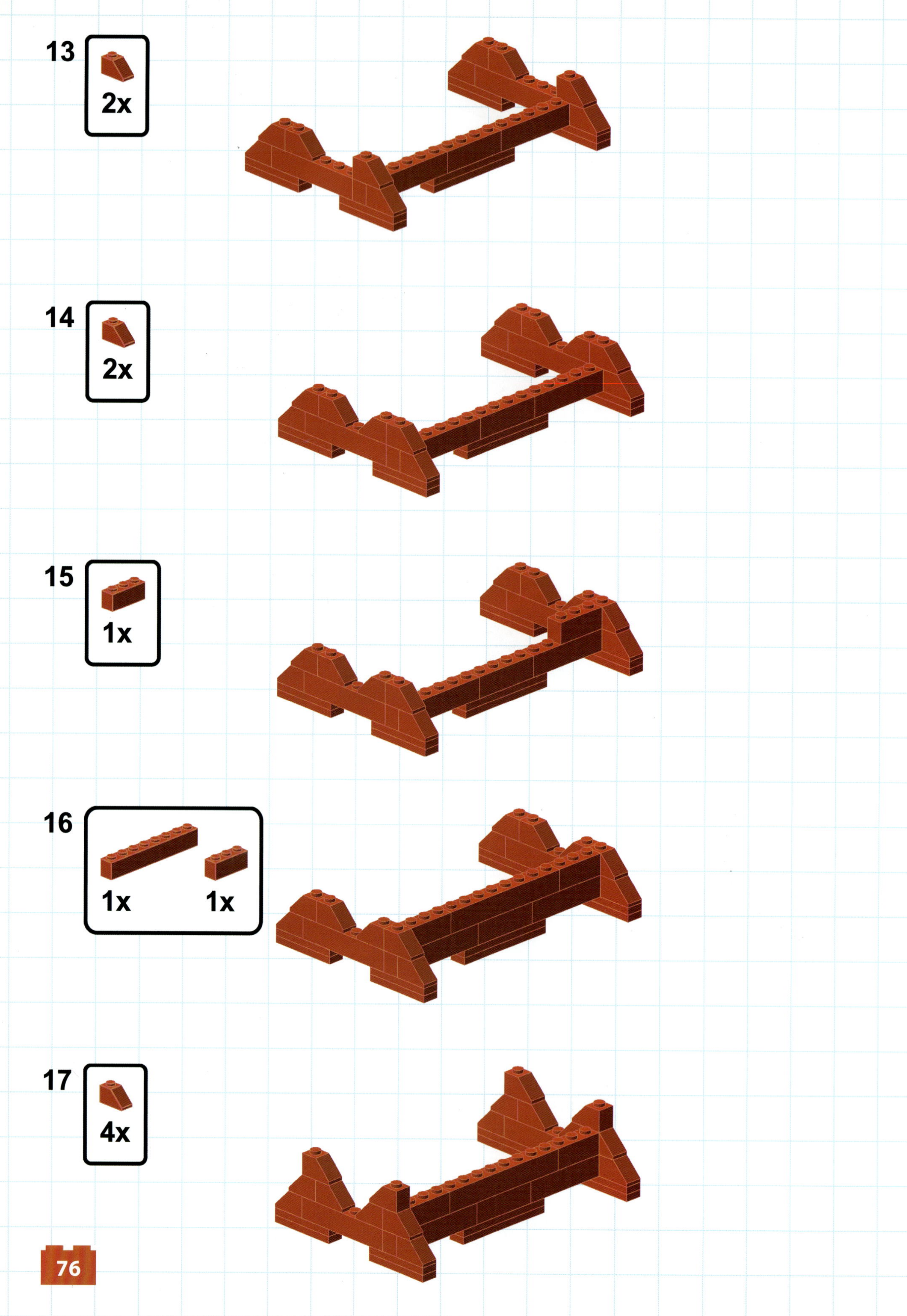
13
2x
14
2x
15
1x
16
1x
1x
17
4x

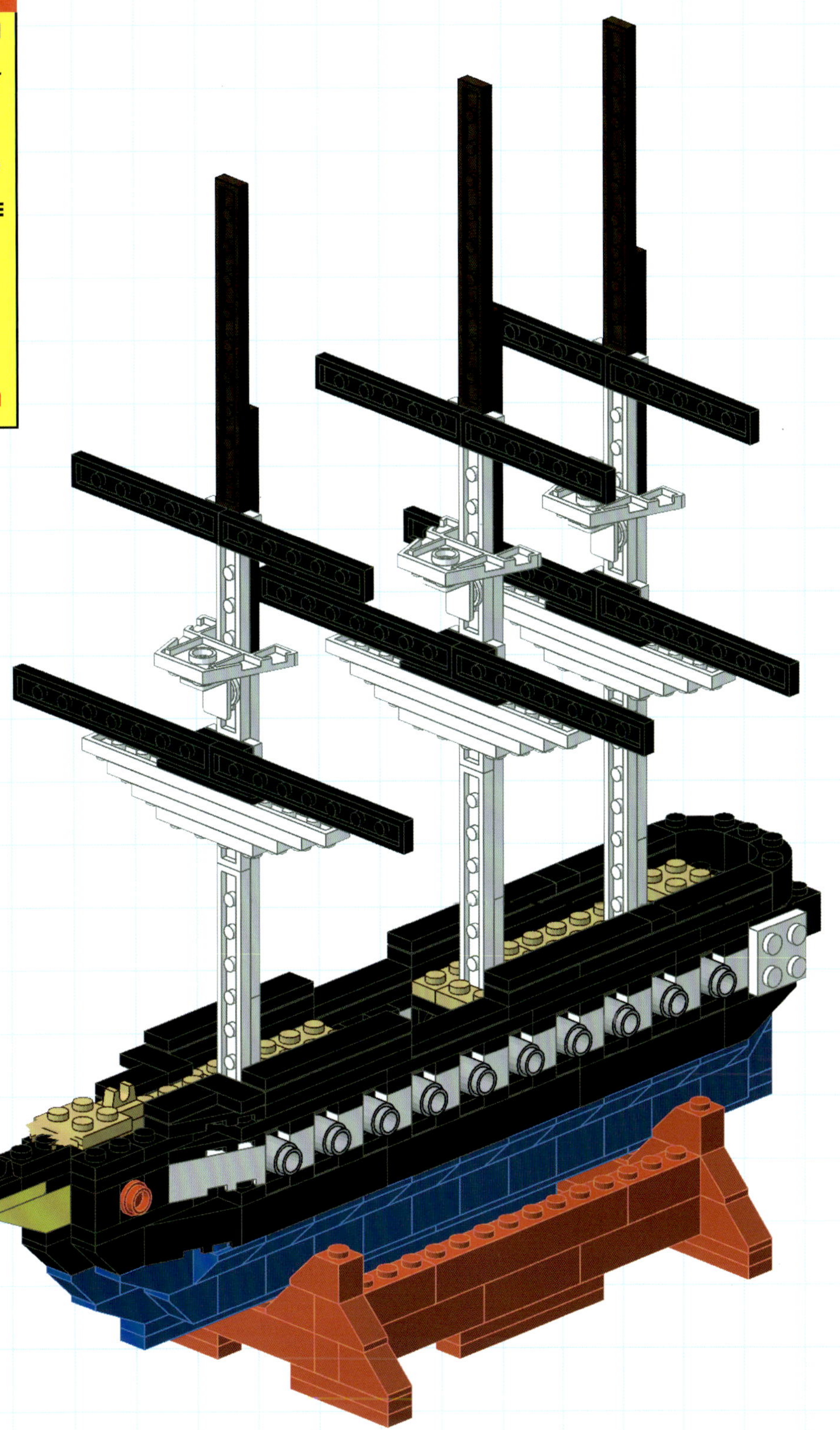

## Ready to take your building to the next level?

## Download a FREE BONUS SET OF "FUTURE CAR" INSTRUCTIONS now!

As a special bonus for purchasers of this book, you can download a **FREE BONUS SET OF INSTRUCTIONS** to build a Future Car at this link:

**http://www.twomorrows.com/media/FutureCar.pdf**

This car takes its inspiration from *Blade Runner* with a touch of *Back to the Future*, and the wheel frame is separate from the car frame, so different bodies can be built to fit the wheels. These detailed instructions were too lengthy to print here, but you can download them now, and enjoy building this more extensive set. It's your FREE BONUS for buying this book!

# SPECIAL OFFER!

## Order a Bundle with *BOOK ONE* of the *You Can Build It* series, including all the parts you need to build a Tulip (111 pieces) and a Spacefighter (71 pieces) for only $20! (*Book One* alone: $10)

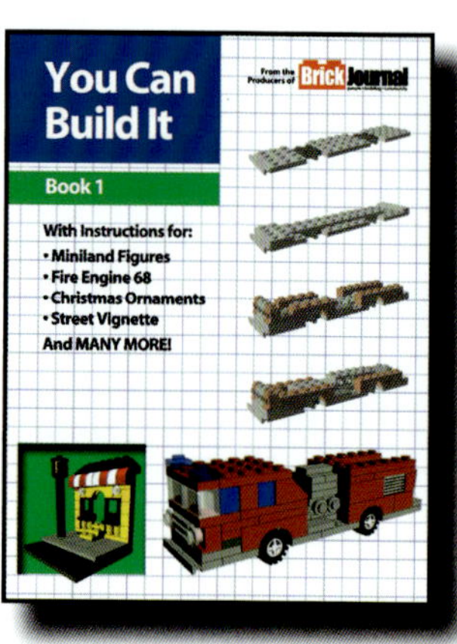


These Limited Edition sets are custom designed by *BrickJournal* editor Joe Meno, and included in *You Can Build It, Book One.* While supplies last, you can order the bundle (book plus two sets) for $20 plus shipping at this link:

*http://twomorrows.com/index.php?main_page=product_info&products_id=1061*

*NOTE: CHOKING HAZARD! Contains small parts. Not intended for children under 3. These are not LEGO® Products. These are re-used LEGO elements that have been repackaged or altered from their original form. LEGO is a trademark of the LEGO Group, which does not sponsor, authorize or endorse this product. The LEGO Group is not liable for any loss, injury or damage arising from the use or misuse of this product.*

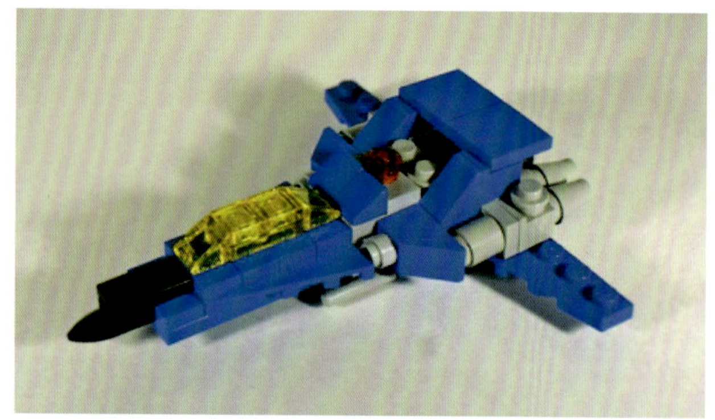

**TwoMorrows. A New Day For LEGO Fandom.**

TwoMorrows Publishing • 10407 Bedfordtown Drive • Raleigh, NC 27614 USA • 919-449-0344 • FAX: 919-449-0327
E-mail: **store@twomorrowspubs.com** • Visit us on the Web at **www.twomorrows.com**

# BrickJournal

people • building • community

## THE MAGAZINE FOR LEGO® ENTHUSIASTS OF ALL AGES!

**DIGITAL EDITIONS AVAILABLE FOR ONLY $3.95**

**BRICKJOURNAL** magazine (edited by Joe Meno) spotlights all aspects of the **LEGO®** Community, showcasing events, people, and models every issue, with contributions and how-to articles by top builders worldwide, new product intros, and more. Available in both **FULL-COLOR** print and digital editions. Print subscribers get the digital version **FREE!**

*LEGO, the Minifigure, and the Brick and Knob configurations are trademarks of the LEGO Group of Companies.*

**PRINT SUBSCRIPTIONS: Six issues $57 US ($75 Canada, $86 elsewhere)**
**DIGITAL SUBSCRIPTIONS: $23.70 for six digital issues**

### BRICKJOURNAL #1

The ultimate resource for **LEGO** enthusiasts of all ages, showcasing events, people, and models! **FULL-COLOR** #1 features an interview with Certified LEGO Professional **NATHAN SAWAYA**, car designs by **STEPHAN SANDER**, step-by-step building instructions and techniques for all skill levels, new set reviews, on-the-scene reports from **LEGO** community events, and other surprises!

(84-page print magazine) **SOLD OUT**
(Digital Edition) **$3.95**

### BRICKJOURNAL #2

This **FULL-COLOR** issue spotlights blockbuster summer movies, LEGO style! Go behind the scenes for new sets for **INDIANA JONES**, and see new models, including an **MINI FLYING WING** and a **LEGO CITY**, a lifesize **IRON MAN**, plus how to **CUSTOMIZE MINIFIGURES, BUILDING INSTRUCTIONS**, a tour of the **ONLINE LEGO FACTORY**, and lots more!

(84-page **FULL-COLOR** magazine) **$8.95**
(Digital Edition) **$3.95**

### BRICKJOURNAL #3

Event Reports from **BRICKWORLD, FIRST LEGO LEAGUE WORLD FESTIVAL** and **PIECE OF PEACE** (Japan), spotlight on our cover model builder **BRYCE McGLONE**, behind the scenes of **LEGO BATMAN**, LEGO at **COMIC-CON INTERNATIONAL, FIRST LEGO LEAGUE WORLD FESTIVAL**, plus **STEP-BY-STEP BUILDING INSTRUCTIONS, TECHNIQUES**, and more!

(84-page **FULL-COLOR** magazine) **$8.95**
(Digital Edition) **$3.95**

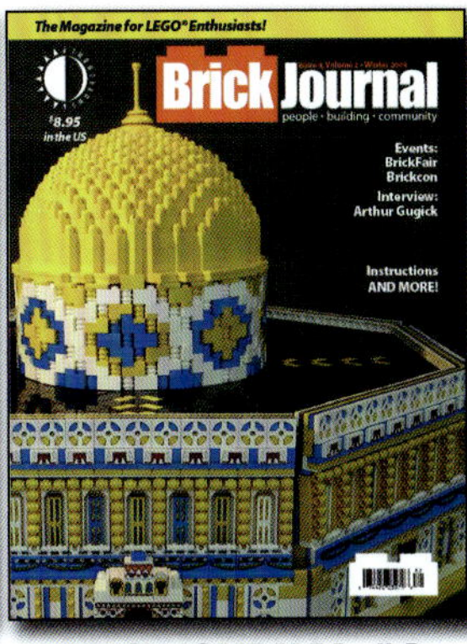


### BRICKJOURNAL #4

Interviews with **LEGO BUILDERS** including cover model builder **ARTHUR GUGICK**, event reports from **BRICKFAIR** and others, touring the **LEGO IDEA HOUSE**, plus **STEP-BY-STEP BUILDING INSTRUCTIONS** and **TECHNIQUES** for all skill levels, **NEW SET REVIEWS**, and an extensive report on constructing the Chinese Olympic Village in **LEGO!**

(84-page **FULL-COLOR** magazine) **$8.95**
(Digital Edition) **$3.95**

### BRICKJOURNAL #5

Event report on the **MINDSTORMS 10th ANNIVERSARY** at **LEGO HEADQUARTERS**, Pixar's **ANGUS MACLANE** on LEGO in film-making, a glimpse at the LEGO Group's past with the **DIRECTOR OF LEGO'S IDEA HOUSE**, event reports, a look at how **SEAN KENNEY**'s LEGO creations ended up on **NBC'S 30 ROCK** television show, instructions and spotlights on builders, and more!

(84-page **FULL-COLOR** magazine) **$8.95**
(Digital Edition) **$3.95**

### BRICKJOURNAL #6

Spotlight on **CLASSIC SPACE SETS** and a look at new ones, **BRANDON GRIFFITH** shows his **STAR TREK MODELS**, LEGO set designers discuss their work creating the **SPACE POLICE** with **PIRATE SETS, POWER FUNCTIONS TRAIN DEVELOPMENT**, the world's **TALLEST LEGO TOWER, MINI-FIGURE CUSTOMIZATION**, plus coverage of **BRICKFEST 2009** and more!

(84-page **FULL-COLOR** magazine) **$8.95**
(Digital Edition) **$3.95**

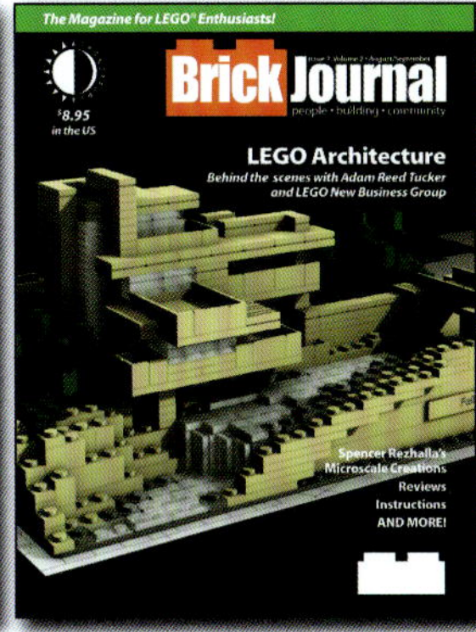


### BRICKJOURNAL #7

Focuses on the new **LEGO ARCHITECTURE** line, with a look at the new sets designed by **ADAM REED TUCKER**, plus interviews with other architectural builders, including **SPENCER REZKALLA**. Also, behind the scenes on the creation of **POWER MINERS** and the **GRAND CAROUSEL**, a **LEGO BATTLESHIP** over 20 feet long, reports from LEGO events worldwide, and more!

(84-page **FULL-COLOR** magazine) **$8.95**
(Digital Edition) **$3.95**

### BRICKJOURNAL #8

We go to the Middle Ages, with a look at the LEGO Group's **CASTLE LINE**, featuring an interview with the designer behind the first LEGO castle set, the **YELLOW CASTLE**. Also: we spotlight builders that have created their own large-scale version of the castle, and interview other castle builders, plus a report on **BRICKWORLD** in Chicago, ands still more instructions and building tips!

(84-page **FULL-COLOR** magazine) **$8.95**
(Digital Edition) **$3.95**

### BRICKJOURNAL #9

BrickJournal looks at **LEGO® DISNEY SETS**, with features on the Disney LEGO sets of the past (**MICKEY** and **MINNIE**) and present (**TOY STORY** and **PRINCE OF PERSIA**)! We also present Disney models built by LEGO fans, and a look at the newest Master Build model at **WALT DISNEY WORLD**, plus articles and instructions on building and customization, and more!

(84-page **FULL-COLOR** magazine) **$8.95**
(Digital Edition) **$3.95**

### BRICKJOURNAL #10

BrickJournal goes undersea with looks at the creation of LEGO's new **ATLANTIS SETS**, plus a spotlight on a fan-created underwater theme, **THE SEA MONKEYS**, with builder **FELIX GRECO!** Also, a report on the **LEGO WORLD** convention in the Netherlands, **BUILDER SPOTLIGHTS, INSTRUCTIONS** and ways to **CUSTOMIZE MINIFIGURES, LEGO HISTORY**, and more!

(84-page **FULL-COLOR** magazine) **$8.95**
(Digital Edition) **$3.95**

### BRICKJOURNAL #11

"Racers" theme issue, with building tips on race cars by the **ARVO BROTHERS**, interview with **LEGO RACERS** designer **ANDREW WOODMAN, LEGO FORMULA ONE RACING, TECHNIC SPORTS CAR** building, event reports, instructions and columns on **MINIFIGURE CUSTOMIZATION** and **MICRO BUILDING**, builder spotlights, **LEGO HISTORY**, and more!

(84-page **FULL-COLOR** magazine) **$8.95**
(Digital Edition) **$3.95**

### BRICKJOURNAL #12

A look at school sculptures by **NATHAN SAWAYA**, builder **MARCOS BESSA**'s creations, **ANGUS MACLANE**'s CubeDudes, a Nepali Diorama by **JORDAN SCHWARTZ**, instructions to build a school bus for your LEGO town, minifigure customizations, how a **POWER MINERS** model became one for **ATLANTIS**, building standards, and much more!

(84-page **FULL-COLOR** magazine) **$8.95**
(Digital Edition) **$3.95**